And You Shall Be a Blessing

Encountering People of Other Cultures and Religions

Ben Naja
Moussa Sy

Bibliographic information published by the Deutsche Nationalbibliothek
The Deutsche Nationalbibliothek lists this publication in the Deutsche Nationalbibliografie; detailed bibliographic data are available in the Internet at http://dnb.d-nb.de.

ISBN 978-3-941750-46-3

© 2011 by Ben Naja / Mussa Sy
2nd edition

VTR Publications
Gogolstr. 33, 90475 Nürnberg, Germany
http://www.vtr-online.com

Cover design: Susanna Hansen
Cover photos: © Matt Brandon

Unless otherwise stated, scripture quotations are taken from the New International Version

Printed by Lightning Source (UK/USA)

Contents

Introduction 5
1 Biblical Basis 7
2 Preparing the Ground 11
3 Past Shortcomings 14
4 The Witness… 19
5 Understanding the Context 28
6 Communicating without Words 39
7 Communicating with Words 61
8 The Big Invitation 89
9 Growing as a Follower of Jesus 95
10 Home Based Fellowships of Faith 112
11 Multiplication 133
Epilogue 137
Appendix 1: The Straight Path –
 an Example of a Contextual Approach to Evangelism 138
Appendix 2: A Short Story for Your Muslim Neighbors 148
Appendix 3: Eight Special Signs Were Given to Seven Major Prophets 150
Appendix 4: Jesus in the Quran and in the Bible 154
Appendix 5: Chronological Bible Study – 44 Studies 156
Bibliography 158
Index of Figures 159
Index of Tables 159

Introduction

Since the beginnings of history, it has been God's aim to bless man. God's first act after creating Adam and Eve was to bless them:

God blessed them and said to them... (Gen 1:28)

When man lost this blessing through the fall, God's great search and salvation program started, aiming at re-establishing fellowship with man. Gen 3:9 reports God's reaction to man's fall: *"Where are you?"* This cry of God's heart is the origin of his divine mandate for whoever follows him. This mandate was not only given to Jesus' followers at the end of his life, neither is it an invention or an idea of the church – it is rather and above all else a divine initiative to bless all human beings and to bring them back to community with him.

This divine desire to bless man and restore fellowship with him reappears in Genesis 12, when God calls Abraham: I will make you into a great nation and I will bless you;

I will make your name great, and you will be a blessing...*and all peoples on earth will be blessed through you.* (Gen 12:2-3)

The Hebrew text would also allow us to translate as follows: *...and all families on earth will be blessed through you."* First through Abraham, then through the people of Israel, and finally through the Messiah and his followers, it was God's will to bless all families on earth. The supreme blessing will be received by all families when they accept in their midst the Blessed, the Messiah, and decide to follow him.

It is therefore not up to the church to convert people of other religions – rather, she is called to be part of this divine initiative, the *Mission Dei*, aiming at blessing all peoples, clans and families on earth. This initiative or divine mandate is not about a big confrontation of religions – rather, it is about being and transmitting blessing to them.

Even today, there are still countless families, clans and people groups who have neither heard nor understood what this blessing is all about. The divine mandate for the church and for every follower of Jesus has always been to share the blessing. Over centuries, this mandate has been neglected.

History shows that when the church neglected to share the blessings or the Mission Dei, God allowed other peoples to penetrate their nations, often attracted by the material blessings of Christian civilizations. This seems to be paralleled by current events. Western Christian nations (as well as Sub-

Saharan Christian areas) are overwhelmed by the massive immigration of all kinds of people from all over the world. This raises many fears. But – could it be that God allows these waves of immigration to bless these very people groups? Could it be that God will, through this immigration, reach his original aim of blessing all families on earth, may be because there is no other way

In any case, this book wants to encourage us to take seriously the divine mandate to bless all families on earth. There are many books which describe the World's religions. We do not want to add one more. Rather, it is our aim to show practical ways to handle today's challenges and expand God's blessing to ever more families.

Ben Naja
May 2009
2nd edition, March 2011

1
Biblical Basis

God invites us to play an active part in blessing all peoples on earth. What a privilege! But before starting anything, we must make sure that we are following closely the perfect plan of God, that we are working according to his will, and that we are following his vision. As far as taking His blessing to all peoples of the earth is concerned, we can build on a solid Biblical base, as this chapter will demonstrate.

The Promise

And I tell you that you are Peter, and on this rock I will build my church, and the gates of Hades will not overcome it. (Matt 16.18)

Jesus himself planned to build a faith community, his Church. He will keep his promises. He will do everything he has said. He is the author and the leader of the Church and he will not allow his plan to bless all peoples to fail. Although history shows that the Church has suffered many setbacks and sometimes almost disappeared, she was always in sure hands. And God will protect it and will ensure that it survives until the final day. He assured his disciples that "even the gates of Hades will not overcome" the church He is going to build. We see this happening today in an unprecedented way.

> For where two or three come together in my name, there am I with them. (Matt 18:20)

As well as promising to build his Church, Jesus also promised his presence. Where two or three disciples meet in his name, the Lord is there. Whatever the size of the faith community, whatever its weaknesses, the Lord is there with it. He is also the One who will make it grow.

Please note that although Jesus speaks here of his Church, he does not mention any *church form* or *church name*. The Greek word for "church" is *ekklesia*, literally "the community of those called out", the community of those who received the blessing in Jesus. This *ekklesia* is not in any way defined by specific forms, denominations or names, but by the community of those who follow Jesus.

The Mandate

> Then Jesus came to them and said, 'All authority in heaven and on earth has been given to me. Therefore go and make disciples of all nations, baptizing them in the name of the Father and of the Son and of the Holy Spirit; and teaching them to obey everything I have commanded you. And surely I am with you always; to the very end of the age.' (Matt 28:18-20)

The natural consequence of the divine promise is a divine mandate. Although Jesus is the real foundation (1Cor 3:11) of the church, and despite the fact that *he* will plant it in the whole world, man has also been given a responsibility. Jesus uses those who follow him as tools in his hand to fulfill his promise.

The Empowerment

> But you will receive power when the Holy Spirit comes on you; and you will be my witnesses in Jerusalem, and in all Judea and Samaria, and to the ends of the earth. (Acts 1:8)

Without divine empowerment it is impossible to carry out the divine mandate. This authority comes to us from the Holy Spirit. The Spirit of God is a Spirit of blessing and therefore also of Good News. Therefore, whoever is filled with him cannot do anything else but expand this divine blessing to other people. The Holy Spirit produces in us a "holy go"! – a go to my neighbor, wherever that might be, so that he also might receive this blessing. The proof that someone is really filled by the Holy Spirit will be that he is in some way dedicated to people in his Jerusalem (people in his immediate neighborhood), in his Judea (people of the same culture), in his Samaria (people in his country, but of a different culture) and to the ends of the earth. The one who is filled with the Spirit cannot do anything else but go and commit himself in some way to this God-sized work of blessing the nations.

The Process

> They preached the good news in that city and won a large number of disciples. Then they returned to Lystra, Iconium and Antioch, strengthening the disciples and encouraging them to remain true in the faith. 'We must go through many hardships to enter the kingdom of God, they said. Paul and Barnabas appointed elders for them in each church and, with prayer and fasting, committed them to the Lord, in whom they had put their trust. (Acts 14:21-23)

The first disciples took the divine mandate seriously. Within a few decades, new communities of believers were planted throughout the then known world.

This passage shows us the three stages of their work:

- *Evangelism*: they preached "*euangelion*", Good News, God's blessing in Jesus Christ, wherever they were.

1. Biblical Basis

- *Edification*: they built up those who had accepted this blessing, and made of them real followers of Jesus. The aim of this process was to plant local faith communities.
- *Establishment*: they appointed local leaders; we believe this was with the aim of healthy growth, both within the faith community and their society.

This book deals with this process of planting new indigenous faith communities. We will return to the various stages all the way through this book.

The Means

In 2Corinthians 11 Paul defends his apostleship with a vivid description of the ways God used him to extend the blessing to the entire then known world:

> Are they servants of Christ? (I am out of my mind to talk like this.) I am more. I have worked much harder, been in prison more frequently, been flogged more severely, and been exposed to death again and again. Five times I received from the Jews the forty lashes minus one. Three times I was beaten with rods, once I was stoned, three times I was shipwrecked, I spent a night and a day in the open sea, I have been constantly on the move. I have been in danger from rivers, in danger from bandits, in danger from my own countrymen, in danger from Gentiles; in danger from false brothers. I have labored and toiled and have often gone without sleep; I have known hunger and thirst and have often gone without food; I have been cold and naked. Besides everything else, I face daily the pressure of my concern for all the churches. Who is weak, and I do not feel weak? Who is led into sin, and I do not inwardly burn? If I must boast, I will boast of the things that show my weaknesses. (2Cor 11:23-30)

We will speak about a lot of methods in this book, but we must emphasize the foundation of them all: that the men and women whom God chooses to do His work must be willing to make sacrifices. Jesus sacrificed himself to bless all families on earth. In the Book of Acts we follow the footsteps of the apostles as they planted many new faith communities. Humanly speaking, the price was extremely high (think of Stephen and many other martyrs after him). It demanded total dedication from the chosen instruments and the willingness to suffer at both a physical and emotional level. *God's ways have not changed: he blesses all families on earth through the sacrifices of his followers.*

The Result

> To the church of God in Corinth, to those sanctified in Christ Jesus and called to be holy, together with all those everywhere who call on the name of our Lord Jesus Christ – their Lord and ours. (1Cor 1:2)
>
> To the churches in Galatia... (Gal 1:2)
>
> To the church of the Thessalonians in God the Father and the Lord Jesus Christ... (1Thess 1:1)

The divine program to bless all peoples resulted in the planting of local faith communities. In Chapter 10 we will discuss the form of these churches in some detail.

The Final Vision

> And they sang a new song: 'You are worthy to take the scroll and to open its seals, because you were slain, and with your blood you purchased men for God from every tribe and language and people and nation.' (Rev 5:9)

The book of Revelations shows us the glorious final vision. Then, both history and church will come to their completion. When all peoples, all families of the earth, will have received the divine blessing in Jesus, the big mandate for the church will no longer be necessary. God's big final goal will then be reached: fellowship with all peoples will be restored, and He will eternally be worshiped. In the final vision, *God's original plan of Eden will become reality: God and man in unity, man finding his highest pleasure and joy in the eternal worship of the Almighty God.* Two main elements are particularly important in this final vision: representatives of all peoples will have accepted God's great invitation – and the Lamb will receive his deserved worship. The sacrifices were worthwhile. There will be no tears anymore. Pain and suffering will no longer exist – a true happy ending.

2
Preparing the Ground

Realize that God is doing a New Thing!

How do we know that God is doing a new thing?

- *More co-workers*: the big problem in early church history as well as today is the lack of laborers. Following Jesus' command (Matt 9:37-38), the believers have prayed for more laborers over the centuries. As a result of this, we see today how millions of co-workers from the Global South (Latin America, Africa and Asia) are joining those from Western nations.
- *More prayer*: Over the last few years, an increasing number of worldwide prayer movements have been started. They focused particularly on the most neglected areas and peoples of the world.
- *More cooperation*: It has become common practice to work in strategic partnerships. Churches and individuals grow in their understanding that the overall *mission dei*, the big divine program of blessing must be highest priority – rather than the promotion of a particular organization or denomination.
- *More contextualization*: the Church has finally understood that the *ekklesia* can and should take on other, more suitable forms in order to be relevant and meaningful in new cultures.
- *More political, social and economic instability*: God shakes whole peoples and nations, economic systems and societies. In such volatile times, when all human securities fall, people tend to seek for more eternal securities.
- *Disillusionment of a growing number of people of other religions.* The growing radicalization and politicalization (e.g. suicide bombers) of certain religions open moderate adherents for the Gospel. For example, more and more moderate, liberal, and disappointed Muslims speak out against the senseless killing "in the name of true Islam", and are turning towards constructive ways of expressing their beliefs.
- *The time of God*: There are various signs on a global level that show: God is now building momentum to extend his blessing to all people groups on earth.

Motivate others to join!

Every church should aim at blessing its surroundings, and particularly people of other cultures and religions. All members of a church can contribute in some way to reach this goal. Every church should set apart a number of its members and commission them with this task, possibly also providing more training for them. They need to make particular efforts to get to know people of other cultures and to work with them in culturally sensitive ways, visiting them, inviting them to their homes and sharing the Good News with them.

Commit to prayer – *much* prayer!

Intense intercession is a first step to bless other people. Individual believers or whole churches can "spiritually adopt" whole people groups and intensively and perseveringly pray for them, until local faith communities are planted among them. Intercession always has consequences for the intercessor. The believer who prays regularly and intensively for a specific people group will over a period of time have an increasing love for it. He will have an increasing burden to physically reach out to them and bless them.

Get training!

Get more training. Working with people from other cultures and religions is a special challenge. For the Good News to be relevant and attractive to them, new communication methods and church forms are required. This is a complex task. Attend workshops and training seminars, read good books on this topic, learn some new abilities.

Understand the context!

Research is never a waste of time! Before communicating the Good News, you need to understand the background and context of those who will listen to your message: their religion, their lifestyle, their culture, their needs and aspirations. Only then will you be able to transmit the Gospel in a relevant way.

You can learn about their context by reading specific books. However, the best way is to spend lots of time with them, having in-depth contacts and friendships with people of that culture.

Establish good strategies!

It is important to define good working strategies prior to starting the actual work. Others have worked before us. Some were very successful, others were not. We can learn from the successes of others as well as from their failures.

2. Preparing the Ground

Not all strategies are useful. That's why we should carefully and prayerfully plan and prepare for our ministry.

We have three basic sources for our strategies: Revelation, Reflection, and Research. The first leads us to Scripture, the second to reasoning, the third to objective (scientific) observation.

Figure 1: The three sources for our strategies

3
Past Shortcomings

In this third chapter, we are going to reflect on the past. It is not our intention to judge past efforts from today's vantage point. When we think of the sacrificial obedience of many of Christ's servants in the face of overwhelming obstacles in aspects of health (many of them dying from malaria within months after their arrival), language acquisition (when hardly any linguistic tools were available) or lack of infrastructure, we can only admire their courage and praise God for their lives. Nevertheless the Church has made certain mistakes. With today's unprecedented resources and progress in many fields we have been given superb benefits that should guide us in not repeating these mistakes. Which mistakes are they?

The Church has neglected people of other cultures

Why has the Church neglected to bless people of other cultures?

- *Lack of access*: Many governments where the most neglected people groups live, do not issue visas and work permits for fulltime Christian co-workers. They are so-called "closed countries." However, the church has finally rediscovered the fact that "spiritual visas" are not necessary to do "spiritual" work in these countries. Even if governments do not issue spiritual visas for Christian co-workers, they can still access them – in most cases as "tentmakers", through their profession or as students. In Biblical times, co-workers like Paul and Peter did not wait for a spiritual visa before getting involved in sharing the Good News. Even without such visas, they were highly effective and not hindered in their ministries in any way.

We also see that nowadays in many nations God is bringing these people right to our doorsteps, so that we no longer have an excuse, especially in regard to the Muslim world: through the massive immigration of people from predominantly Muslim countries during the last decade or so, most Muslim people groups are accessible in Europe (e.g. France, UK) and other countries. Areas which in the past had practically no Muslims, now have a good representation of people of that faith, e.g. in certain cities in France and England, or in West African places like Abidjan, Lagos, Accra and many others. In addition, through globalization it has become much easier to emigrate into Islamic countries (particularly Middle Eastern countries) and find jobs there.

3. Past Shortcomings

- *Lack of focus in mobilization*: the Church has concentrated on other fields which were considered more receptive and more open to the Gospel. This is indeed understandable from a result – or success-driven approach, but sadly has led the Church to overlook or sideline others.
- *Lack of visible and quantifiable success*: the Church has often had a false idea of success, based on results rather than obedience. Especially in Muslim areas there was not much visible success. Many concluded that these people groups should therefore not be a priority. However, only the Holy Spirit can bring about revelation and visible "results". *The messenger has basically done his part each time a Muslim has heard the Good News in a way which is clear, easily understood and culturally adapted – even if s/he does not choose to follow Christ.*
- *Lack of vision*: generally the Church has found it difficult to spiritually and financially support co-workers who do not produce visible fruit. It is a matter of concern that at times even workers with a clear calling for people groups without the Gospel are being entrapped by church activities and thus prevented from reaching beyond the Church.

The Church has not respected the will of God

The Bible clearly tells us that the divine blessing will expand to all people groups:

- *The blessing of Abraham will spread to all the families of the earth*
- The LORD had said to Abram, 'Leave your country, your people and your father's household and go to the land I will show you. I will make you into a great nation and I will bless you. I will make your Past shortcomings 13 name great, and you will be a blessing. I will bless those who bless you and whoever curses you I will curse; and all peoples on earth will be blessed through you. (Gen 12:1-3)
- *All are included in God's call to repentance , no-one is condemned to perish*
- The Lord is not slow in keeping his promises as some understand slowness. He is patient with you, not wanting anyone to perish, but everyone to come to repentance. (2Pet 3:9)
- *God wants all men to be saved*
- … who wants all men to be saved and to come to a knowledge of the truth. (1Tim 2:4)
- *The sacrifice of Jesus is for all men*

- He is the atoning sacrifice for our sins, and not only for ours but also for the sins of the whole world. (1Jn 2:2)
- *There is only one mediator between God and men: Jesus Christ*
- For there is one God and one mediator between God and men, the man Christ Jesus. (1Tim 2:5)

Too often and for too long has the Church understood the word of God to say that blessing is for the Church. However, if you read the Bible with open eyes, you will soon come to the understanding that whoever has received God's blessing is immediately called to pass on this blessing to others.

- *Our love for the Lord is measured by our obedience to his word. Jesus said,*

    If you love me, you will obey what I command. (Jn 14:15; 15:10)

    What, among others, was his command? Go into all the world...all creation. (Mk 16:15)

- *No-one can believe in the Good News of Jesus Christ without having heard it*

    How, then, can they call on the one they have not believed in? And how can they believe in the one of

    whom they have not heard? And how can they hear without someone preaching to them? And how can they

    preach unless they are sent? As it is written, 'How beautiful are the feet of those who bring good news!' (Rom 10:14-17)

- *In eternity, every people group will be represented before the throne of God*

    After this I looked and there before me was a great multitude that no-one could count; from every nation, tribe, people and language, standing before the throne and in front of the Lamb. They were wearing white robes and were holding palm branches in their hands. And they cried out in a loud voice: 'Salvation belongs to our God, who sits on the throne, and to the Lamb.' (Rev 7:9-10)

    And they sang a new song: 'You are worthy to take the scroll and to open its seals, because you were slain and with your blood you purchased men for God from every tribe and language and people and nation. You have made them into a kingdom and priests to serve our God and they will reign on the earth.' (Rev 5:9-10)

Research shows that there are still several thousand people groups or clans without a local faith community. The vast majority of them are Muslim. Although this context presents special challenges and difficulties, it must become a priority for the Church.

3. Past Shortcomings

The Church has retreated

In some countries, *fear* of Islam has gripped the Church. Instead of approaching Muslims in an attitude of love and compassion in order to share the Good News with them, some Christians have retreated in fear or are seeking unnecessary confrontation. This is especially true for nations where there has been a massive immigration of Muslims. It is true that the Islamic religion grows rapidly. The Muslim population grew from 150 million in 1900 to one billion in 1994. Today, in the year 2011, there are about 1.6 Billion Muslims, approx. 23 % of the world's population.

It is true that Muslims are often in the news, especially because of their extremism, and that they claim rights even where they are a small minority. And it is true that there are examples of a painful past for the church, such as for example:

- Slavery – Muslim people groups have taken people as slaves. Many of these former slaves are Christians today. How do mainland-Tanzanians feel about their Zanzibar neighbors today? What is the natural reaction of the Chichewa speaking churches in Malawi towards their Yao neighbors today?
- Civil wars – many Christians in Nigeria, Southern Sudan, and other parts of Africa and Asia (e.g. Indonesia) have lost their homes, had their churches burnt more than once, or lost friends and relatives at the hands of Muslim soldiers, or violent mobs. Unless they can find healing and the power to forgive they will not be able to meet Muslims in the love of Christ.

We see *political or economic exploitation* (a government which has favored Islam at the expense of the Christians) and an *increasing and aggressive immigration* of Muslims in traditionally Christian areas.

However, our reaction to all these facts should be neither aggressive confrontation nor fearful retreat. Our reaction should be compassion which expresses itself in the communication of the best message the world has ever heard. Their massive immigration in formerly Christian areas or countries should therefore not be seen as a threat, but as an opportunity. It is a god-given opportunity to no longer neglect them, but rather to share the blessings with them, now that they are our neighbors.

The divine law of sowing and reaping (cp. Gal 6:7) is also valid in this context: wherever there is little sowing, there will be little harvesting. We can only expect that many Muslims will accept Jesus' big invitation when many hear this message in an understandable and culturally sensitive way. On a global level, this is happening more and more: In our generation, more Muslims have decided to follow Jesus than ever before.

Therefore, we see on one hand that the challenges are overwhelming. On the other hand, we also see that the divine blessing in Jesus is being extended to an ever increasing number of people groups and individuals. May be Paul's description of his ministry in Ephesus describes our situation today. He wrote:

> ...because a great door for effective work has opened to me, and there are many who oppose me. (1Cor 16:9)

The Church has used unsuitable methods and approaches

Unsuitable methods and strategies have hindered Muslims in understanding and accepting the Good News. They have not accepted the Gospel, not because of the "scandal of the cross", but because of the "scandal of the Church" and because of the "scandal of our methods." We should not put up unnecessary barriers because of our culture or our way of doing things that will then hinder others to hear our message.

More recent research has shown that *the main reason why Muslims do not follow Jesus is not on the doctrinal-theological, but rather on the socio-cultural level.* It is tragic, if our cultural habits, our way of living our faith, or our non-sensitive methods, hinder others to accept the very message we try to transmit.

Here a few examples:
- Light Western clothing of women
- Confrontational, aggressive or even offensive way of communicating
- Unusual forms for worship or church
- Non-sensitive eating- and drinking habits.

These things or habits might not be sinful per se. However, when we aim at expanding the blessing to people of other cultures, we have to do it in a sensitive way.

4
The Witness...

In the following chapters, we will speak a lot about methods and strategies to succeed in our ministry of blessing all people groups. However, as this ministry is first and foremost done through relationships, we will first focus on the person of the witness and consider a few characteristics that will qualify him.

...has the right perspective

We often base our perspective on wrong or unstable foundations. Examples for such foundations are our own negative experiences or negative experiences of others, prejudices or unbelief. The best foundation for our perspective is the Word of God.

If we base our perspective on our feelings or experiences, we are soon going to abandon the work. Our perspective must be based on what God has said, because that is the only truth. When we are immersed in the work, perhaps feeling tired and discouraged, we must step back and understand all over again what God sees, to see as He sees, to think as He thinks – *to have God's vision for our lives and ministries.*

Psalm 2 is an important passage to show us God's perspective. You might wonder what Psalm 2 has to do with the peoples on earth? It speaks of perspective. Many Christians see in Muslims a threat and withdraw in fear.

> The kings of the earth take their stand and the rulers gather together against the LORD and against his Anointed One. 'Let us break their chains,' they say, 'and throw off their fetters.' (Ps 2:2-3)

In the Qur'an, there are about forty Christological verses or titles that reflect Biblical teaching. For example, in the Qur'an, Jesus is presented as a sinless prophet, the Word of God, the Messiah, a healer, someone who raised the dead, the son of Mary or the one who will come back at the end of times. There are also two teachings that are not coherent with the Bible: Jesus did not die on the cross, and Jesus is not the Son of God. Of course, these two truths, that Jesus did die on the cross and that Jesus is the Son of God, are foundational to our faith and salvation.

This is like a plot against the Lord and his Messiah, and many Christians do not know what to do in relation to this threat. But verse 4 glances at the heavenly places and the perspective changes completely:

> The One enthroned in heaven laughs; the LORD scoffs at them

The Lord is not intimidated by anything in any way. He does not feel threatened. What does he do in view of this human threat? He laughs! Many Christians feel intimidated – but Got is sovereign, and he only allows that will finally serve His glory and the best for man. He is the Almighty, he was, and is, and will ever be on his throne. Despite all human impossibilities, despite all difficulties, he was able to bless the peoples even under the Communist Regimes and finally brought them down. He can and will do it also in all other human systems and religions of this world.

We must have God's vision. He is on the throne and he always will be. If we want to be effective in our ministry, we must have an unshakable faith in the sovereignty of God. The witness who feels intimidated or threatened will not feel free to approach people from other cultures – or will seek unnecessary confrontations.

The psalmist goes on and says:

> I have installed my King on Zion, my holy hill. I will proclaim the decree of the Lord. He said to me: You are my Son. (Ps. 2:6-7)

God Himself has established his Son as the eternal King. Even if many reject Him and do not believe in him as the Son of God – he nevertheless *is* the Son of God, because God wanted and decided it this way. It is not the Christians who said that Jesus was the Son of God, but God himself.

> Ask of me, and I will make the nations your inheritance, the ends of the earth your possession. (Ps 2:8)

The nations, all the nations, including the hardest, are Jesus' legitimate and God-given possession.

In the New Testament, we read that those who are in Jesus are his co-heirs:

> Now if we are children, then we are heirs – heirs of God and co-heirs with Christ, if indeed we share in his sufferings in order that we may also share in his glory. (Rom 8:17)

In other words: In Christ, the nations, *all the nations*, are our legitimate inheritance in the spiritual realm. This spiritual truth should encourage and inspire us. Instead of being intimidated or fearful, we should have this perspective and know that it is our legitimate right to extend Christ's blessing to all peoples on earth. The following end vision shows that this will one day become reality.

> You are worthy to take the scroll and to open its seals, because you were slain and with your blood you purchased men for God from every tribe and language and people and nation. You have made them into a kingdom and priests to serve our God and they will reign on the earth. (Rev 5:9-10)

4. The Witness

One day, representatives from all tongues, nations and people groups will have accepted the blessings in Jesus and share eternity with him and his followers. Do we really believe what is written here, or do we trust more in our negative experiences and feelings? Many quickly get discouraged because they do not have in the depths of their hearts a strong faith that God will do all that he has said.

Therefore, the divine mandate is not first and foremost the great commandment. It is first and foremost the great *promise*, the privilege of being part of the great plan of God and his great program to bless all nations.

To have the right perspective means also to read world history and world events with the right eyes. The big chapter on the end times, Matthew 24, is probably one of the darkest passages of Scriptures. Here we read of natural disasters and wars, of anarchy and destruction. However, in the midst of this darkness we read that the Good News will be known among all peoples. Then, and only then, the end will come.

To have a divine perspective, therefore, means to accept that many people, possibly whole nations will only open themselves up for the Good News in the midst of or after these disasters and catastrophes. God may allow these human disasters, but when he does that, it is always with the goal of finally blessing and redeeming people.

…has the right attitude

What feelings do you have when you look at the many immigrants in your city or region? What do you think when you hear again of a suicide bomber in the Middle East? Do you have feelings of anger, resignation or bitterness? We are quick to have prejudice and stereotype views of people from other cultures and religions.

However, we should have the attitude of Jesus when facing the crowds:

> Jesus went through all the towns and villages, teaching in their synagogues, preaching the good news of the kingdom and healing every disease and sickness. When he saw the crowds, he had compassion on them, because they were harassed and helpless, like sheep without a shepherd. Then he said to his disciples, 'The harvest is plentiful but the workers are few. Ask the Lord of the harvest, therefore, to send out workers into his harvest field. (Mt 9:35-38)

Most people in the crowds were Jews. Didn't Jesus know the Jews? Didn't he know that a few months later these same Jews were going to shout, "Crucify him, crucify him"? Of course Jesus knew these things. He knew the Jews. During his whole ministry, the people that gave him most problems were the

Jews. They rejected him. Despite this, he loved them. He was filled with compassion for them. He loved them so much that he was even willing to die for them. This and only this is the right attitude: love them in spite of everything, love them to death.

Are we filled with love or hate? Do we have the heart of God for people or a heart of flesh? Do we see the people with our eyes or with the eyes of God?

If we see people with God's eyes, suddenly we no longer see blind fanatics, terrorists or extremists – we rather simply see people; people without a shepherd; people who really are in desperate search of that shepherd. Could they possibly be so fanatic and extreme because they actually don't know this shepherd? *Sharing Good News is actually nothing else than taking other people's hands, whoever they might be, and leading them to the Good Shepherd.* And this is the deepest need of every human being on earth, whether they realize it or not.

If we have this great love of God in our hearts, we can also really forgive everything that causes us to suffer or has caused us to suffer in the past, and we can then accept and love them the way they are. And this is the most important condition to really be able to meet and serve them.

Jesus knew exactly what the hearts of these Jews were like. He knew that they were going to reject him and make him suffer. But he knew also that they were like sheep, lost without a shepherd, deceived and roughly handled. And he had compassion on them.

What do you see, when you look at them? Do you see threatening people or desperate sheep who need a good shepherd?

…has his personal security in God

Fear paralyses us. The love of God for others sets us free. We need courage to overcome our fears and intentionally be witnesses of the Good News. We need courage to approach people of other cultures and religions. Many workers, also those sent to other nations, retreat. They are fearful. And many don't have any meaningful contact with the very people they came so far to bless. Sometimes, instead of integrating themselves into the community, messengers have formed a ghetto of Christians. They have traveled hundreds or even thousands of miles with the aim of blessing other peoples, but they have not succeeded in getting past the last few feet or inches.

We can only approach people of other cultures in a meaningful way, if we know who we are and what we have in Jesus Christ. We must meditate on passages such as Ephesians 1 to better understand our position in Christ. These truths give us security. We desperately need this security when people of other cultures and religions question our faith and our values. They might even ridicule, reject or sideline us. If I do not have full security in Christ, forgiveness of sins, assurance of eternal life, and also total protection from every attack from the occult and from witchcraft, I will always be afraid that something might happen to me or that I will be destabilized.

The word of God encourages us:

> For God did not give us a spirit of timidity, but a spirit of power, of love and of self-discipline. (2Tim 1:7)

...has a real burden

We have already spoken about Jesus and his deep love for the crowds and even for the people who hated him. We will now see how the apostle Paul was burdened for the people he wanted to bless:

> I speak the truth in Christ – I am not lying; my conscience confirms it in the Holy Spirit – I have great sorrow and unceasing anguish in my heart. For I could wish that I myself were cursed and cut off from Christ for the sake of my brothers; those of my own race... (Rom 9:1-3)

From the book of Acts and Paul's epistles, we know that Paul had been persecuted, beaten, stoned and rejected by the Jews. Several times, they actually tried to kill him. In spite of all this, he says, "I would rather be separated from Christ than see my brothers perish." Do we have this burden for Muslims? Would you be willing to be cut off from Christ rather than see Muslims perish?

Paul wrote the following:

> Brothers, my heart's desire and prayer to God for the Israelites is that they may be saved. For I can testify about them that they are zealous for God, but their zeal is not based on knowledge. Since they did not know the righteousness that comes from God and sought to establish their own, they did not submit to God's righteousness. Christ is the end of the law so that there may be righteousness for everyone who believes. (Rom 10:1-4)

Paul's wholehearted desire and prayer to God was that "they may be saved". Just like the Jews, Muslims also have zeal for their law and religion. They seek salvation through keeping laws and rules. They try to establish their own, human righteousness, a righteousness that will never be sufficient before God, because it will always be human and therefore imperfect. Only Christ as the only perfect human being that ever lived can perfectly fulfill God's law, and therefore only those who trust in him can fully be righteous before God.

If we have such a love, such a burden for our people group, we will also be totally dedicated to them and to our mandate of bringing blessing to them. We will then do whatever it takes to bring Good News to them, whatever it costs, at any price. Many say that they cannot advance because they lack the means, the time or the capacity. But if all our being is consumed by this vision, we cannot do otherwise – we must go! *Life with God is not a career – it is a passion!*

How can we cultivate this burden? The more we pray and intercede for these people, the more love and burden for them will grow in us. The more we get to know the people, their needs and problems, their challenges and bondages, the more we will have a burden to offer them the fresh water of the Gospel.

…lives in complete dependence on God

This dependence on God will in particular be evident in the following two areas:

- He is a person of prayer and fasting, exercising a ministry of intercession

The word "Jihad" is very popular today. The word of God also speaks about war and weapons, but in the New Testament, they are exclusively spiritual. It is never our task to fight people in the natural realms – rather we are in a constant battle with the powers which are behind them.

> For our struggle is not against flesh and blood, but……against the spiritual forces of evil in the heavenly realms. (Eph 6:12)

Ephesians 6 speaks to us about our weapons in this spiritual battle. They are not human or physical but spiritual. The passage finishes by a call to prayer:

> And pray in the Spirit on all occasions with all kinds of prayers and requests. With this in mind, be alert and always keep on praying for all the saints. Pray also for me, that whenever I open my mouth, words may be given me so that I will fearlessly make known the mystery of the gospel, for which I am an ambassador in chains. Pray that I may declare it fearlessly, as I should. (Eph 6:18-19)

We are in a battle against spiritual powers and forces. Therefore, our battle is never against people which really are nothing else than deceived victims of these powers. Rather we are in a battle against the one who has blinded millions of people:

> The god of this age has blinded the minds of unbelievers; so that they cannot see the light of the gospel of the glory of Christ, who is the image of God. (2Cor 4:4)

They can never understand the message of the gospel without the revelation of God and without this veil being lifted from their eyes. Only God can do this. That's why prayer is so essential to our ministries:

4. The Witness

> The weapons we fight with are not the weapons of the world. On the contrary, they have divine power to demolish strongholds. We demolish arguments and every pretension that sets itself up against the knowledge of God, and we take captive every thought to make it obedient to Christ. (2Cor 10:4-5)

Prayer and intercession are the most important element of our service to other people. In our ministry to people of other religions, we must understand that the conflict is above all a spiritual one. As a result, our most important activity must also be spiritual. This is particularly the case if we work with Muslims who follow a mystic form of Islam (Sufism, Popular Islam). For them, faced with the message of the gospel, the question is not, "Is it true?" but "Is it more powerful?"

In such contexts, a message is not evaluated with the intellect, but rather with life. The question will not be whether a teaching is true or wrong, but rather whether it has the power to change daily life. In this context, prayer for the sick and oppressed will be crucial.

Muslims pray five times a day their ritual prayers. In addition, many of them also practice the more personal *"Dua"* prayer. To what point are we prepared to dedicate ourselves to prayer? Are you ready and willing to invest more time and energy for this crucial activity?

In relation to prayer we must also review our practice of fasting. Is fasting a regular practice in your spiritual life? Moses fasted forty days and nights. Jesus knew extended times of prayer and fasting. The Early Church fasted twice a week. Discipline of our bodies and submission of our wills to God equip us for service. Are you ready to pay this price?

Given the importance of prayer, fasting and intercession for people of other cultures and religions, these activities should also become a high priority in our churches, fellowships and cell groups.

- *He lives in the power and under the direction of the Holy Spirit*

This work will never be done without the help of the Holy Spirit:

- He will give us the courage and the strength to approach and love other people.
- He will give us the right words at the right time
- He will give us divine encounters with people we do not know, but who have been prepared for years to receive the Good News
- He will act supernaturally by dreams, visions and healings and he will give us every other spiritual gift necessary for the work
- He will convict them of their sin

- He will lift the veil from their hearts and reveal the truth concerning Jesus Christ.

…has perseverance

If someone wants to work with people of other religions, he will need perseverance. Only in rare occasions will there be quick success like "instant coffee".

This perseverance will be evident in patience (Rom 5:3-5) and endurance (Heb 10:35-39). Many co-workers abandon their ministry quickly because they are easily discouraged if they don't see quick visible results of their efforts. But whoever wants to bless people of other religions has to be willing to invest many years, possibly a lifetime. He will learn language and culture. He will build meaningful relationships. He will lovingly and patiently share the Good News of the Gospel. He will have to overcome deceptions and disappointments. Considering all this, he will need a good portion of *determination and commitment* in order to go on for years without abandoning the work.

We should be careful not to confuse the words "success" and "fruit." The word "fruit" is mainly used in the New Testament for our character. It would contain areas such as love, humility, discipline or patience. It is our task to transmit the message with as much patience, love, cultural sensitivity and wise methodology as ever possible – but it is God's task to give revelation.

Many co-workers among Muslims have abandoned their work because they have not understood these truths. We need perseverance in order to reach the goal. It would be a pity to stop praying and serving these people just because what we had hoped for has not yet become reality.

…is ready to make sacrifices

Most of us desire to live out the experiences of the NT, particularly those of the Gospels (healings, miracles) or of 1Corinthians 12 and 14 (gifts of the Holy Spirit). However, we tend to forget that pain and suffering are part of the basic New Testament experiences. Just think of Christ's suffering or of Paul who describes his carrier in 2Corinthians 11 and 12 and says: "*I have suffered more than all of you.*"

The Church often preaches a falsified Gospel. It forgets that wealth, health and peace are not the equivalent of blessing. There are various examples in both the Bible and church history which show that often, people who were particularly blessed and close to God were those who suffered most. This is of course particularly true for Jesus and the first apostles (of whom 10 died as martyrs). And in our quest for justice we tend to forget that life is neither just nor fair

4. The Witness

for most people on earth and that they can do nothing about it (e.g. people under totalitarian regimes or in war zones).

Jesus sends us into the world as he has been sent by his Father. He said that all men will hate us because of him (Lk 21:17). Paul adds that all those who want to live a godly life in Christ will be persecuted (2 Tim 3:12). The Greek word for "witness" in Acts 1:8 is *"marturios"* or in English "martyr". It can mean "blood witness". Some who are sent will never again return to their earthly home. Our readiness to make sacrifices should reach the point that, when we are sent to foreign nations, we are willing never to come back. Many people of other religions take serious risks when they decide to follow Jesus. They might be persecuted, ridiculed, insulted, possibly even beaten or mistreated. The witness has to be ready for the same risks and sufferings.

We should not only be ready to die for him, but also to live for him. In an anti-Christian context, living for him can even be more difficult than dying for him. It could for instance mean to be isolated, ridiculed and offended over years, possibly over a lifetime. Jesus was able to bear the many sufferings because he had the eternal joy set before him. We, too, can be ready for any sufferings because this same eternal joy has been promised to us.

> Therefore, since we are surrounded by such a great cloud of witnesses; let us throw off everything that hinders and the sin that so easily entangles, and let us run with perseverance the race marked out of us. Let us fix our eyes on Jesus, the author and perfecter of our faith, who for the joy set before him endured the cross, scorning its shame, and sat down at the right hand of the throne of God. Consider him who endured such opposition from sinful men, so that you will not grow weary and lose heart. (Heb 2:1-2)

5
Understanding the Context

If we want to have any meaningful contact with people of other cultures and beliefs, we have to understand where they are coming from, what their preoccupations, needs and problems are. The Bible says:

> My dear brothers, take note of this: everyone should be quick to listen, slow to speak and slow to become angry... (James 1:19)

Have you ever meditated on the fact that God has created us with two ears and two eyes but with only one mouth? Could it be to show us that we should listen and look well before we speak? It is only when we understand people well that we will be able to speak with assurance and relevance.

Therefore, even nominal, non-religious Muslims are still Muslims culturally and socially. Even though they do not follow the Islamic Religion, their cultural and social identity is still Muslim, and they would therefore consider themselves as Muslims.

We first have to understand that although Islam is a Religion, it is also much more than a Religion. Islam is also a Community, and Islam is also a Culture. Actually, there are many Islamic Religions, many Islamic communities and many Islamic cultures. Islam seeks to embrace all areas of life.

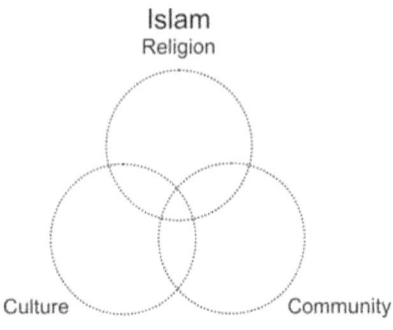

Figure 2: Islam is more than Religion

Understand their social and intellectual context (Islam as community)

At a *social level*, the Muslim is surrounded by three important social groups represented by three circles: The nuclear family, the extended family, and the

5. Understanding the Context

Ummah. If the messenger comes from a Western background with its extreme individualistic society, he has to understand that a Muslim does not view himself first of all as an individual, but as a small part of a large community. In many non-Western languages, there are very detailed terms describing the relationships with an extended family – most of these expressions do not even have an equivalent word in Western languages. This shows the enormous importance that the social construction and the extended family have in those cultures.

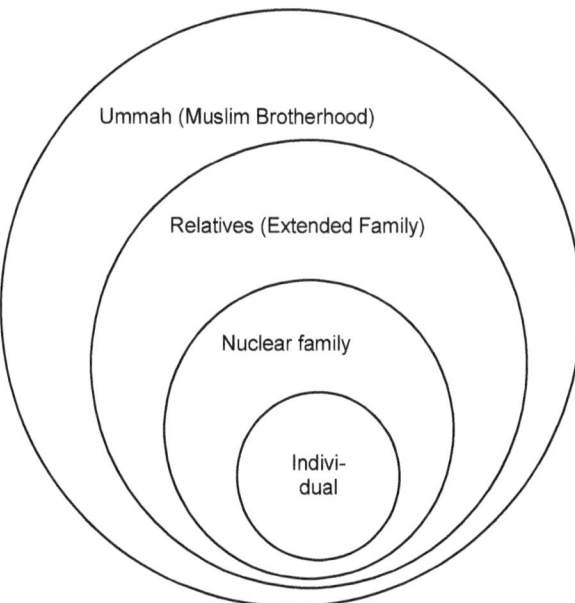

Figure 3: Their social context

The individual Muslim is surrounded by an entire clan and a worldwide brotherhood. Every decision must be made in agreement with the community in order to maintain harmony. The one who leaves the *ummah* is seen as a traitor. One is born as Muslim, and his whole identity is defined by Islam – whether he likes this or not. To be a Muslim is only rarely the result of a personal decision. It is more about being part of a group of relatives, a society and belonging to a people group. In many Arab contexts, to be an Arab means to be a Muslim. The person who no longer wants to be a Muslim loses also the right to be Arab and must therefore be expelled or eliminated. In chapter 10, we will explore ways for such people to be followers of Jesus and remain in their cultural setting. The Ummah has a *worldwide* (the worldwide community of all Muslims) and a *local* dimension (the local community of all Muslims at an ethnic or village level). Most Muslims are much more affected by the local dimension of the Ummah.

At an intellectual level, a Muslim has three major influences which determine his thoughts and his actions:

- *Classical Islam*, based on the Qur'an and the Hadith (Islamic tradition). Every Muslim is obliged to adhere to these beliefs.
- *Popular beliefs*: belief in a mystical, supernatural spiritual world. This second level includes elements of popular beliefs such as the fear of the Jinn (evil spirits), the evil eye and curses; as a result, it also includes the search for protection through charms and magic, traditional healing methods etc. In everyday life, this second influence might be stronger than the first.
- *His personal convictions and experiences*: in Islam there are at least as many sects and groupings, views and opinions as there are in Christianity. All Muslims do not share the same convictions or religious practices. For instance, there are the very strict Wahabis, and the liberal Sufis who, in certain contexts like Egypt worship Allah with drums and guitars. Still other sects only pray three times instead of the usual five times. The Shiite sect is of course again a completely different branch of Islam.

This leads us to our next section, the individual context.

Understand their individual context

As we mentioned in the previous section, we have to understand that Islamic society is in no way a single world in which everyone thinks and believes the same thing. To speak about the different Islamic sects or schools law is not a part of this book. But we do wish to speak about the different types of people and how to approach them:

The different types of people and how to approach them		
Type	Characteristics	How to approach him
Fanatical, Extreme	- likes discussions - likes to question our faith - seeks to convince	- pray a lot - if possible, keep up friendly contact - try to avoid confrontation - do not seek pointless arguments
Intellectual, Educated	- likes reading, educating himself - likes constructive debates	- give him good literature - since he likes debating, organize debates on established facts

5. Understanding the Context

Disillusioned, disappointed	- discouraged by the fanaticism of others - has a lot of questions, is open to something new	- offer him the good news, the living water - approach him through real life testimonies
"Spiritual", focused on the supernatural	- does a lot of "dua", fasts often - seeks after supernatural experiences	- pray with him for supernatural revelations - show him the stories of the appearances of angels and miracles in the Bible
Nominal Muslim, Non practicing	- does not pray, does not go to the mosque - does not know much about Islam - may be marginalized and isolated	- approach him in a social way - he needs a friend - help him to understand that Islam is not the only religion - there are other options

Table 1: The different types of people and how to approach them

A better knowledge of the individual's context helps us to use more suitable strategies and, therefore, transmit a more relevant message.

Understand their faith (Islam as Religion)

What we just said about the individual's context is also true for their whole belief system: the better we understand it, the more we are familiar with their faith and religious practices, the more relevant our message can become. Here is a short summary:

- *The basic beliefs of a Muslim (Iman):*
    - Allah: the oneness of Allah (112:1-4)
    - The angels of God (35:1) and the good and evil *Jinn* (spirits)
    - The books of God (2:136): Taurat, Zabur, Injil, Qur'an
    - The prophets of God (35:24). According to the Islamic tradition, there are 124,000 prophets, of whom 25 are mentioned in the Qur'an (22 of the 25 also figure in the Bible). In the Islamic theology, prophets are first and foremost "warners".
    - The day of judgement (21:47)
    - Predestination (25:2)
- *The obligatory practices of a Muslim: the Five Pillars of Islam(Din)*
    - The confession of faith (*shahadah*)

- The five daily ritual prayers (*salat*)
- Almsgiving (*zakat*): a contribution of 2.5 % of annual revenue
- Fasting during the month of Ramadan (*sawm*): the 9th month of the Muslim calendar, the month of revelation
- Pilgrimage to Mecca (*hajj*) for whoever is in good health and has sufficient means
- Holy war (*jihad*): Islam only speaks of five pillars, but certain Muslims consider Jihad as a 6th pillar. Jihad is not only war, but can also mean effort (9:5; 6:29).

In *Popular Islam* a multitude of practices coming from animism and the occult are added to these beliefs and practices. Here are some examples:

- Drinking the ink with which Qur'anic verses have been written on wooden slates
- Trusting in talismans and charms Understanding the Context 33
- Bringing offerings and blood sacrifices to get *baraka*, God's blessing
- Fear of the evil eye
- The magic use of numbers and number combinations
- Seeking *baraka* at the tombs of holy men (*pirs*)

Understand their cultural background (Islam as Culture)

Culture can simply be understood as "the way that we do things here." Culture describes areas such as religion, language, social institutions (marriage, family, community practices).

There are several reasons for us to think about culture:

- *Before speaking about doctrines and faith, we are going to meet people in their culture.* This is inevitable, because religion is always part of the culture and is immersed in it. We can never meet someone outside of his culture. If we are not sensitive to the culture, we put up pointless barriers that may close the hearts and minds of people before we even open our mouths to speak.
- Although the Gospel in itself is non-cultural, it must always be expressed in cultural forms. If we understand people's culture well we can explore ways through which the Gospel could be expressed in it.
- We must distinguish between the Gospel and the culture. *We are not called to bring a new culture, but to implant the Gospel seed into their hearts and then let it blossom within the culture of a given people group.*

Here are some of the main traits of culture that matter to most Muslims:

5. Understanding the Context

- *Family life*
    - Marriage and family are very important and expected from all members of the society.
    - The world of men is usually strictly separated from the world of women.
    - Family is defined as extended, not as nuclear.
    - It is expected that children obey their parents, older siblings, uncles and grand-parents.
- *Food*

The Islamic religion distinguishes between "halal" (clean, allowed) and "haram" (unclean, forbidden) food and beverages. Examples for things that are haram are:

- animals, which have died a natural death or because of illness
- pork
- blood
- animals that were not slaughtered ritually, meaning without invoking the name of Allah
- alcoholic beverages
- eating with the left hand

- *Clothing*
    - Especially women are expected to clothe very conservatively (however, the context defines what is conservative – for example, there can be huge differences between rural and urban areas)
    - As a general rule, modesty and simplicity are expected.
- *Symbols and language*
    - Arabic symbols, art and language are essential for all Muslims
    - The Qur'an is basically untranslatable into other languages. It must be studied and recited in Arabic.
    - The most important religious terms are also untranslatable in other languages – all Muslims therefore have to pray in Arabic and use Arabic religious terminology.

- *Worship and religious life*
    - No artistic representation of humans or animals is permitted.
    - Most Islamic sects do not authorize musical instruments or singing in the mosques (except rhythmic repetitions Qur'an verses).
    - In mosques, there is no furniture except for the member (pulpit). To worship, Muslims do not sit on benches, they rather use mats or carpets.
    - The Qur'an is a holy book. Muslims honor it; in Popular Islam they even revere it. They put it in the highest place in a room, and in court, they swear on it.
    - The feasts ("Eid") are important parts of Islamic culture. The most important is the Feast of the Sheep (Id-al Kabîr), when a sheep is killed in remembrance of Abraham's sacrifice.
- *Social life*
    - Muslims greet each other by saying "*Salamu Aleykum,*" which means "Peace be with you." The answer to this greeting is "*Wa aleykuma Salam*", "and peace be with you". This greeting is very close to the Hebrew "*Shalom*" and the "peace-greeting" of the early church (cp. Lk 24:36b).
    - Good relationships with neighbors and relatives are very important. The individual must be integrated into the group. The interest of the group is considered as more important than the interest of the individual.
    - There is no difference between the secular and the sacred world. Islam is a totalitarian religion that encompasses every part of life.
    - Most Islamic cultures are shame oriented. Honor of one's people, religion and family must be maintained at any price.
    - Everyone is expected to show great respect for the elders or for everyone who is older than himself.
    - Hospitality is a basic characteristic of most Islamic cultures. In nomadic society it is almost a sacred obligation.
- *Some general remarks*
    - The best way to learn the culture of people is to spend lots of time with them, to visit them and to welcome them in our

5. Understanding the Context

homes, to observe them, to ask questions and to listen to them. This is also the best way to rectify mutual prejudices.

- It would not be fair to generalize too much. An "Islamic culture" does not exist because Muslim people groups already had their culture before embracing Islam. In addition, cultures change from country to country and even within a country, from region to region. Also, Islamic cultures are adapting to modernism and in many urban settings, an urban youth culture develops that has less and less in common with traditional Islamic values.

- Having studied the culture of a people group, we have to look at ourselves again. What will they think of our way of doing things? What may be shocking for them? In what areas should we be more sensitive and behave in more appropriate, culturally adapted ways?

Understand their prejudices

It is important to understand that there are mutual prejudices between Christians and Muslims. Muslims hold at least as many if not more prejudices against Christians as Christians hold against Muslims. When we work among them, we do not begin with a clean slate on which we can construct our biblical structure. In fact, in approaching them, we find that a whole structure already exists – lots of things have been "constructed" before us and in fact against us. Consider these:

- *Doctrinal prejudices concerning Biblical Christology*
    - The Christian Trinity is perceived as God the Father, Mary the Mother and Jesus the Son (Surah 5:116)
    - Jesus is construed as the physical Son of God. Muslims usually think that Christians believe God was united with a woman to father Jesus (Surah 112.1-4; 6:101)
    - Jesus had only a human nature just like every other descendant of Adam (Surah 5:75)
    - Jesus was created by God (Surah 3:59)
    - Jesus did not die on the cross, but was raised to heaven without dying (Surah 4:156-158)
    - Islamic tradition says that after his return to earth, Jesus will reign for some forty years, will get married and will father

children. He will die and be buried at Medina. On the Day of Judgment he will be raised to life again and will stand before God to be judged along with other men.

- o   Jesus predicted the coming of Muhammad (Surah 61:6).
- • *Prejudices concerning Christians*
    - o *Christians are immoral, capitalists, liberal and alcoholics.* As there is no distinction between the spiritual and the secular in Islam, Muslims assume the same is true in Christianity. But it is the so-called "Christian" countries that produce and spread immoral films and publicity. In many towns in West Africa most bars and brothels are in so-called "Christian" districts. This is seen as a further proof that Christians approve and practice these things.
    - o *Christians have corrupted the Bible.* I have a friend who was told since his childhood that the hand which touches the Bible of the Christians will burn in the fire of hell!
    - o *All Christians are polytheists* who worship three gods (Surah 5:72-73)
    - o *The general behavior of Christians is not respectable*: their style of dress, their way of worship (music and dancing, men and women together, sitting down to pray etc.).

We will speak in Chapter Six about our non-verbal witness. Many Muslims have never met an authentic follower of Christ who really lives out his faith in every area of life according to biblical norms. An authentic Christian witness lived out among them will rectify many of their prejudices.

Understand their needs and their questions

The Good News is only *Good* News when it responds to the felt needs of a person and offers a solution to real problems and answers to relevant questions. Even the best meal is not appealing for someone who is not hungry at all! We should therefore be able to proclaim the Good News as really being the Good News. A Good News which is not only good for us, but which is really good *for them.*

We must treat our contact as a person with questions and concerns and not first and foremost as a member of some religion or other. After all, they are people with desires and needs, just like us.

Before communicating the Gospel, we must do some research to become familiar with their needs, their problems and their questions. It is not only a question

5. Understanding the Context

of knowing how the Gospel meets our needs. We must also know what the *real* felt needs of our contacts are. To identify that, we must get to know them and learn what preoccupies the depths of their hearts. Jesus did this by spending lots of time with people, by getting to know them deeply, and then he had a message of Good News for each individual in his specific situation.

The following table fits primarily into the context of Popular Islam. We recommend you get to know your people very well and then establish a similar table adapted to that context.

Felt Needs	Responses	Solutions offered by the Gospel
Fear of evil; fear of evil spirits and spells; fear of being possessed by demons	Sorcery, amulets, exorcism	Protection through trust in Jesus and his sacrifice, freedom from evil spirits and demons through prayer in the name of Jesus; Jesus has power over evil; the angels of God (Mk 16:17; Jer 27:9).
Fear of the future	Divination, fatalism	Biblical promises; Trust in the Lord of the future; words of prophecy (Is 45:20-21).
Shame culture: loss of honor	Magic, curses, revenge	Real forgiveness and reconciliation are possible; restoration of honor possible also without revenge; full acceptance in the community of the family of God (1Cor 12:27; 2Cor 6:17-18).
Sicknesses	Magic healings, medicine and traditional massage	Prayer (free of charge) in the name of Jesus, laying on of hands, divine healing (James 5:14; Mk 16:17).
Powerlessness of the individual	Search for "baraka"	Power of the Holy Spirit; we are already blessed in Christ with every blessing; prayer (Eph 1:3; Acts 1:8).
Fear of death, eternal separation from God	Prayers and sacrifices for the dead	Victory over death, assurance of eternal life (1Cor 15:54-56; Phil 1:21; Jn 5:24).
Doubts concerning forgiveness of sins	Countless repetitions of formulas ("*istarfurallahi*"), sacrifices	Assurance of forgiveness and true peace possible by the sacrifice of Jesus Christ; the sacrifice of Jesus is valid for everyone and for all time (Jn 1:29; Rom 8:1; 1 Jn 1:9).
A distant God	Sufism, search for the supernatural, dreams, pilgrimage to Mecca	God our Father, Jesus our elder Brother, the Holy Spirit our Comforter living in us; direct access to God (Heb 4:16; Acts 17:30; Is 55:6; Rev 3:20).

Felt Needs	Responses	Solutions offered by the Gospel
Bonds of sin and bad habits	Performance of external rituals (ritual washing, ablution)	Full freedom in Jesus Christ, sanctification, fruits of the Spirit (Gal 5:1, 22-23; Jn 8:32, 36).

Table 2: An example of felt needs

We all agree that "sheep graze where the grass is greener." It is *our* responsibility to show other people where the best grass is. If we do not tell them, they might not be aware that there are actually other, better options for them out there. The more we spread this Good News, the more likely it is that people will understand their real needs and open themselves up for real, eternal solutions.

A closer look at the Table above shows that the felt needs are found a lot more at an emotional-experiential level than at a cognitive intellectual level. Therefore, the point of contact is often not the intellect, but the experience of the power and the presence of God.

In considering the teaching of Islam about Jesus, we see that there is high respect for him as a guide, a healer, as one who blesses, raises the dead etc. He is not exalted for his intellectual knowledge, but for his authority and his power. We can present Jesus in this way, particularly with the aim of establishing initial points of contact.

Jesus *did* take care of the felt needs of those around him. He actually used them to lead people a step closer to him. The apostles followed this example. In Colossae, where Gnosticism was widespread, Jesus was preached as the supreme Wisdom and Knowledge. In Corinth, Jesus was preached as the supreme power, and the Gospel as a Gospel of power.

These facts can help us to identify *"fertile ground for the Gospel"* in the lives of Muslims. Although Jesus came to bring "life to the full" (Jn 10:10), the ultimate need of every individual is forgiveness of his sin and assurance of eternal life. Jesus came to save that which is lost.

In meeting them, therefore, we must understand that Muslims are being prepared in two ways:

- *From a negative point of view*: their prejudices about Biblical Christology and Christians.
- *From a positive point of view*: their unmet felt needs and unanswered questions.

Knowing these two points will help us to understand Muslims better and to share with them a message of *real blessing*, truly *Good News*.

6
Communicating without Words

Introduction 1: The cycle of communication

In the following two chapters, we will discuss many communication strategies and techniques. However, we should never forget that we deal with human beings, not with objects. Therefore, there are no recipes on how to bless other people. Each human being and each situation are different. We can find principles, but applications can only be found in each specific situation and under the direction of the Holy Spirit.

We see communication as a basic cycle that involves four elements:

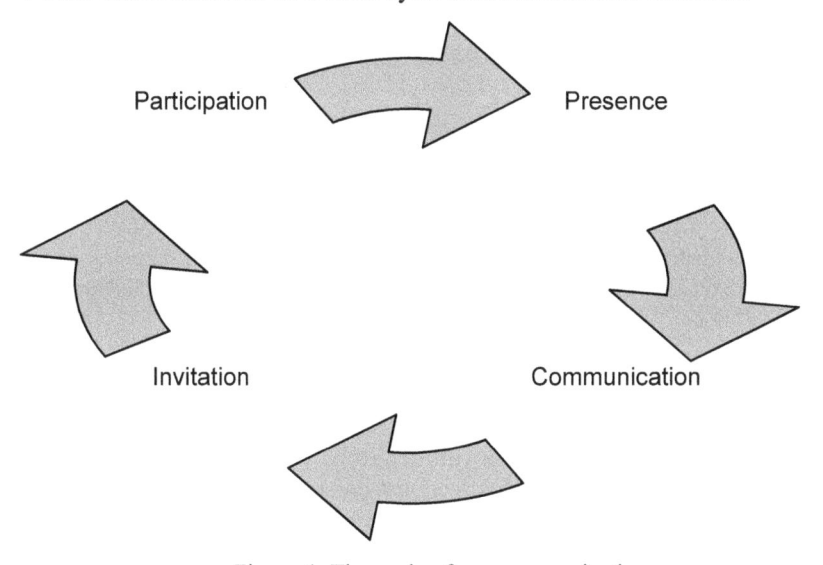

Figure 4: The cycle of our communication

- **Presence**: Communication without words – the wordless witness of an authentic follower of Jesus
- **Communication**: Communication with words of biblical truths about the Messiah
- **Invitation**: Invitation to other people to follow Jesus
- **Participation**: active commitment of the new believer in the work of communicating the Good News.

This cycle must always be repeated:

> And the things that you have heard me say in the presence of many witnesses entrust to reliable men who will also be qualified to teach others. (2Tim 2:2)

In this chapter we are going to discuss the first phase of the cycle, communicating without words. Think of all the chapters you have read up to this point as being preparations for building a house – drawing plans, clearing the ground etc. Now this chapter, communicating without words, is the foundation for the house. The foundation is never an end in itself but without it the building is not viable – so communicating without words is a key, a foundation, from which to build.

Introduction 2: Contextualization

Contextualization is the translation of the unchangeable content of the Gospel into verbal forms that are relevant and meaningful for the people in a specific culture and context.

Biblical examples of contextualization

- *The example of Jesus*

Jesus did not come into the world by chance. He was sent by God with a specific mandate. This mandate was "to seek and to save what was lost" (Luke 19:10). Philippians 2 shows us the method Jesus used to accomplish his mandate:

> ... He made himself nothing, taking the very nature of a servant, being made in human likeness. And being found in appearance as a man, he humbled himself and became obedient to death – even death on a cross! (2:7-8)

That is an example of contextualization – perfectly modeled by Jesus Christ. He did not stay in heaven and preach the love of God from there. No, Jesus was born and was educated as a Jewish child. From outward appearances, nothing distinguished him from other children of his time. When he became an adult, he was a normal citizen of first century Palestine. In his lifestyle, nothing distinguished him from his contemporaries: his words, his food and drink, his clothing, his work and his cultural behavior were the same as those of everyone else. He lived, he suffered and he died as a man.

But from inward appearances, he was fundamentally different from his contemporaries: He was the Son of God, without fault, without sin, in permanent communion with his Father. He shared all of his life with people but without sin and without hypocrisy

His contextualization was so perfect that even his enemies could not distinguish him from other people: to trap him, they needed the betraying kiss of Judas, one of his closest friends (see Lk 22: 47-48).

6. Communicating without Words

- *The example of the apostle Paul*

Cultural adaptation was one of the basic principles for the apostle Paul. The "classic" passage on Paul's methodology is 1Corinthians 9:19-23. This passage does not just show us different methods, but also the aim and the reason for all biblical contextualization.

> Though I am free and belong to no man, I make myself a slave to everyone, to win as many as possible. To the Jews I became like a Jew, to win the Jews. To those under the law I became like one under the law (though I myself am not under the law), so as to win those under the law. To those not having the law I became like one not having the law (though I am not free from God's law but am under Christ's law), so as to win those not having the law. To the weak I became weak, to win the weak. I have become all things to all men so that by all possible means I might save some. I do all this for the sake of the gospel that I may share in its blessings. (1Cor 9:19-23)

Here are some principles:

- *The basic position*: Paul is free in regard to everyone (19a)
- *The specific roles* which Paul adopted:
    - He makes himself the servant (slave) of all (19b)
    - He is like a Jew with the Jews (20)
    - He is like a Proselyte with the Proselytes (20, "under the law")
    - He is like a Gentile for the Gentiles (21, "without law")
    - He is weak with the weak (22a)
    - He has made himself everything for everyone (22b)

The aim of all contextualization: "… to become all things to all men that I might save some" (22c). The word "save" is the key term in this passage: it appears no less than 5 times. If we speak about contextualization, it is about the burning desire to lead lost sheep into the fold of the Good Shepherd.

The reason for all Biblical contextualization: "I do all this for the sake of the gospel that I might share in its blessings". We do not need to change our approach simply to conform to a new methodology, but only if it makes the message of the Gospel clearer to our listeners.

In summary, we can say that both Jesus and Paul exercised a contextual ministry with the one aim of accomplishing the divine mandate on their lives to expand God's blessing to new cultures.

- *The biblical mandate for contextualization*

We have a biblical mandate to follow these examples:

> As the Father has sent me, I am sending you. (Jn 20:21b)

We are all sent into the world as Jesus was sent by his Father. What does that mean? The Scriptures call us to follow the model of Jesus: "Your attitude should be the same as that of Christ Jesus." (Ph 2:5). This attitude of unconditional love, this mindset of deep humility pushed him to live as a normal Jew two thousand years ago. This same attitude of divine "agape" and real humility are so crucial for a witness of the Gospel. Like Jesus, we should adapt ourselves externally to our host culture, while not taking part in their sin. We are also called to follow Paul's model:

> Follow my example, as I follow the example of Christ. (1Cor 11:1)

The Scriptures exhort us to follow the models of Jesus and Paul; in other words: we do not just have a biblical foundation which justifies contextualization; we also have a biblical mandate for contextualization: we are called to a culturally appropriate behavior and lifestyle and to a culturally sensitive way of communicating God's message.

God and culture

One day, God will be glorified and worshipped in many languages, in many cultures, in many different styles (Rev 7.9). Unfortunately, because of transgression, every culture has been affected by sin. As a result, today no culture is perfect.

It is our job to distinguish in our own culture elements that are neutral or opposed to the essence of the Gospel message. These culture specific elements can become unfortunate obstacles, when we invite people of other cultures to accept Jesus' invitation.

We are mandated by God to invite people of all cultures to follow Jesus. However, in this process, they do not have to become like us. This was actually the big topic of the first church council in Acts 15. At that time, the Christian leaders finally decided that people from non-Jewish background did not have to become Jews in order to follow Jesus.

Avoid unnecessary cultural obstacles

All too often we may irritate people from another culture unintentionally even before any verbal communication has taken place. As we saw in the previous section, Paul made every effort to avoid a confrontation of cultures so that people could really listen and accept his message. If Paul lived and worked with Muslims today, what would he do? – He would become like a Muslim to Muslims and invite them to follow Jesus in culturally appropriate ways. Although we do not become Muslims in the religious sense of the term (e.g.

6. Communicating without Words

converting to Islam) we can become *like* Muslims culturally. In the same way Paul did not become pagan, but *like* a pagan, in order to win them.

Most people are culturally blind: we think and believe that our way of doing things and our worldview are the best. Too often we feel superior to others. In order to bring Good News to people of other cultures, we must let go of our cultural arrogance and pride and be willing to appreciate and value others. Other cultures are not less good or less effective – they are simply different!

At the religious-spiritual level, too, we have convictions, habits and practices that are simply our way to do things, without being required by the Gospel or Scripture. They might be allowed by the Gospel, but not required. The problem starts where in our cultural blindness we put these rules and regulations on the same level with Scripture. All too often, these secondary questions then create unnecessary conflicts and confrontations when we work with people of other cultures. Here a few areas in which we should try to avoid unnecessary cultural obstacles:

- *Learn the language: the every-day language of the people*

Jesus and Paul had an advantage in relation to today's messenger as they learned the language of their contemporaries from childhood. However, this does not excuse us. In fact, learning the language is perhaps the most important factor if we want to reach their hearts. *Learning the language of the people we seek to reach with the gospel is in itself a powerful message of our love and respect for them.*

Language acquisition has lots of benefits. The more we understand and speak the language of our neighbors:

- *the less cultural stress we will have when we are in contact with them*
- *the more people will feel honored, loved and valued*
- *the more we will be accepted, find open hearts and an entry into their community*
- *the easier the message will be accepted by them*

A message for the heart will find more acceptance when delivered in the heart language.

Learning a language is not primarily a question of gifting, but of determination and endurance. The best way to learn a new language is to spend lots of time with the local people in everyday life. If you find it hard to learn the language well, try to get at least the basics.

Learn the language: Religious terminology

We already discussed the importance of the Arabic language. For a Muslim, the religious key terms are untranslatable into other languages: they must be uttered in Arabic, whether the individual Muslim understands it or not.

For the witness this means that he/she can overcome a verbal cultural obstacle if he/she knows and uses some Arabic key-terms. Some important expressions are salaam = peace, alhamdulilah = Praise God, or Allahu Akbar = God is great. We are all familiar with the word "Allah", God. The basic confession of faith of every Muslim starts with "la illaha illala....", which means "there is no god but Allah". This has resulted in countless debates in Christian circles. Is Allah the biblical God, or is it just an Arabic idol? – A short look at the history and theology will shed some much needed light in this regard. Please consider that:

- Before the coming of Muhammad, there were already Arabic-speaking Christians on the Arabian Peninsula. They prayed to Allah, the Father of Jesus Christ.

- Today, Millions of Christians in North Africa and the Middle East do not know any other name for God apart from Allah, and they worship him as the Creator of Heaven and Earth and Father of Jesus Christ.

- In many translations of the Bible (not only in Arabic versions) "Allah" is the most common term used for God.

- Hebrew and Arabic are related (Semitic) languages and have the same linguistic roots. "El" and "il" are the basic root forms for God respectively (cp. Mark 15:34 – Jesus calls to "Eloi, Eloi" – which seems to be very similar with the Arabic "illahi, illahi").

- The problem is not the term per se, but the understanding, the content, or the concept, we have of it. In other words: the problem is not whether Allah is God, but rather how we understand Allah. Muslims do not pray to an idol or a false god – they simply have a different and incomplete understanding about who he really is. For instance, they do not perceive that he has a spiritual Son called Jesus Christ.

- In the same way, our forefathers had a very incomplete understanding of the God we worship today. However, this fact was for the first messengers among them no reason to introduce a new term or name for "God" – they rather taught the biblical understanding about God, among other things that he had a Son called Jesus Christ. The most common term used for God in the Greek New Testament is "Theos" (Zeus). In Greek mythology, Zeus, although presiding over the Greek Olympian pantheon, was also the god of the sky and thunder who had siblings, was married and fathered children. The Greek understanding was not even close to the Biblical understanding of God. Nevertheless, this pagan term for God was used by Paul and others and filled with the Biblical concepts and content.

6. Communicating without Words

- *Conclusion*: The term "Allah" is simply Arabic – it is not Islamic per se. Jews, Christians and Muslims worship the same God – however, they differ considerably in how they understand this God. In Arabic, there was and is no other term for "God" than "Allah".

Besides the term "Allah" there are other Arabic words that we should know and use in order to avoid irritation.

Christian Term	Meaning for Muslims	Culturally appropriate term
God	Simply a Christian term	Allah
Jesus Son of God	The physical Son of God	Isa al-Masih (Jesus the Messiah), Nabi Isa (Jesus the prophet), Isa Ibn Meryam (Jesus son of Mary)
The Holy Spirit	The angel Gabriel	The Spirit of God
Christian	Infidel	Believer, follower of the Messiah
Church	A building	The people of Allah, the people of Isa al-Masih, a place of prayer, the faith community (Jamaat)
Gospel	A book corrupted by Christians	The Injil

Table 3: Culturally appropriate vocabulary

Remember the basic principles of contextualization: to use terms and forms that are meaningful and relevant for the people we seek to bless. Our habitual forms and terms are therefore not wrong in themselves. However, in order to remove the highest number of barriers possible, it is important in any cross-cultural setting, to speak their common language with their common terminology and in their normal cultural forms.

- *Adopt a respectable style of dress*

It is a shock to many Muslims when they see the dress code of so-called Christians, especially women. According to the Qur'an, Muslim women must dress respectably and rather conservatively – for their own protection, but also in order to not tempt men. In their context, this means to cover their hair with a veil. Shoulders and knees must always be covered. The strictest sects demand that the face is also covered from the age of puberty. If a Christian lady does not pay attention to her dress code, she can be considered immoral or as having loose morals. This will just confirm their prejudices and make effective communication more difficult, if not impossible. Women who work in foreign countries with Muslims should dress like respected women dress in that society. In many contexts, this means to wear long robes and a veil. Women in Western countries who seek to be in regular contact with Muslim women should avoid dressing in a way that could be considered as provocative. Of course, this applies just as much to men! Wouldn't it be wonderful, if the following story would be repeated in the lives of many servants of Christ?

> As usually I put on local clothes and went out to make new contacts. Walking around and praying the Lord showed me a local store. I greeted the shop-keeper in his language and asked him if he was interested in reading a book in his own language. The book was about how Muslims can learn more about Jesus. The shop was full of charms for protection against evil spirits and evil people. The shop-keeper was very surprised that as an obvious foreigner I was able to speak his language fluently, yet was dressed like the local people. He said to me: "I don't know what this book is talking about, but because you are wearing our clothes and are speaking our language I will read the book." About six weeks later I went back to visit this man again. When I entered the shop I was very surprised that I didn't see any charms left in the whole shop. I asked him what had happened. He said to me: "The book that you gave me changed my life, I am following Jesus and he is my security now." The key to reach this man was both through the language and the appropriate way of dressing.

- *Have a respectable social behavior*

Here is some advice:

  o Respect the Islamic gender separation: if you are a man, don't try to have an in-depth relationship with Muslim women and vice-versa. Avoid looking into the eyes of a woman. In certain contexts, it is not even advisable to greet a woman.

  o Avoid the use of your left hand for eating, giving or receiving a present or money etc.

  o Never show someone the sole of your foot or shoe.

  o Take off your shoes when you enter their houses, when you visit a mosque or when you sit on a mat.

  o Be aware that some Muslims are afraid of the "evil eye." This is why you normally don't admire a beautiful house or a baby in good health. This could be interpreted as jealousy or envy, and it might well be associated with the "evil eye".

  o Respect the social structure of the Muslim society in which elder people, parents and uncles have much more weight and authority than in Western cultures. Don't destabilize their social system; bring honor to parents and older people. For those in foreign countries, it is imperative to underline just how important it is to always have the necessary respect and honor to all those in a position of authority (Sheikhs, Imams, Marabous, local chiefs etc.).

- *Respect their cultural practices and their local customs*

Most cultural practices and local customs do not present any problem to the witness. We can observe them, ask questions about them, evaluate and practice them ourselves. Only when they are in clear contradiction to the written word of God should we distance ourselves from them. This could for instance be the case with occult practice such as magic formulas or charms.

Our eating and drinking habits are a particular area in our adaptation to the intercultural contact with Muslims. On the one hand this means not building unnecessary cultural barriers by eating or drinking what is haram to them. On the other hand, it means following Jesus' advice (Lk 10:8) to eat all that will be presented to us – even though it might be unusual or new to us.

- *Don't invite Muslims to a Christian Church service*

This advice might surprise you. Isn't it our aim to bless all peoples? Indeed, it is. Yet, for a Muslim, participating in a formal Sunday morning service might not be helpful, especially at an early stage; too many things might be surprising, even shocking or unacceptable to him: The way we worship God (with instruments of music, dancing, shouting), the way we furnish our church building (furniture, pictures), the way men and women interact freely in God's house (no separation), the way believers dress in this holy place (permissive, shoes on), the way God's Holy Book is treated (they may conclude that it is not honored when it is put on the floor, amid or even under other books, when they notice verses that are underlined, highlighted, etc.). These are all factors that will only confirm prejudices of Muslims. We will discuss better ways of blessing Muslims in the following chapters.

In concluding this section, we want to emphasize that the main obstacles in our contacts with Muslims are not at a theological level, but much more at a cultural level. It is here that most conflicts and hurts occur. It is also on this level that we have failed most. It is so unfortunate when Muslims cannot accept the blessing in Jesus because of the cultural blindness and arrogance of his messenger. It is on these issues we can and must change. We should remove all manmade barriers that hinder Muslims in accepting Jesus' marvelous invitation.

If we live in a culturally adapted and appropriate way, Muslims will respect us. And this is the first step in our communication of the Good News. *It is not possible to share the Good News if the messenger as a person is bad news.* They will not listen to someone they do not respect. That's why, it is important for the witness to live in a culturally respectable way so that people respect him. Therefore, although it is not our most important mandate, it is nevertheless a crucial step on our way to bring God's blessing to all peoples.

Be hospitable and accept hospitality

In most cultures, good relationships and friendships go "through the stomach". Sharing a meal together can even be like a seal on a contract or an agreement. To be hospitable, to eat and drink together, and the informal fellowship in a family setting are therefore all essential elements in our work.

Jesus and the disciples knew about the importance of hospitality. They often spent time in the homes of their friends. They ate and drank with people from a great variety of cultures and environments: Pharisees, tax collectors and sinners. Jesus knew how important eating together was for his ministry. He did not only visit them in their homes, but also welcomed people where he stayed (e.g. Nicodemus in John 3:2). Eating and drinking with all kinds of people was foundational to Jesus' ministry. On the basis of his own example, he gave his followers this advice:

> When you enter a town and are welcomed, eat what is set before you. (Lk 10:8)

Hospitality should go both ways: not only should we invite people from other cultures into our homes, but we should also accept *their* hospitality. If someone expresses or implies that he does not like someone else's food, he is communicating a message of rejection. Food is much more than simply keeping one's body in good health. The type of food and the way in which it is eaten are part of a given culture. Rejecting it therefore not only means rejecting the food, but also rejecting the people who like it.

The Bible exhorts us to be hospitable (Rom 12:13b). Hospitality is a biblical order *and* a pillar of most Muslim cultures. Therefore, it should also be a pillar of our work.

For co-workers who live in foreign countries, it is important to find out exactly how hospitality is lived out in that particular context. Eating habits and kinds of food vary from region to region. In some contexts, hospitality can also mean to spend a few days with people in a village or to welcome friends from a village in one's home. The result of this will be in-depth relationships.

Are we allowed to eat meat of animals which have been slaughtered in the name of Allah? Muslims always call on the name of Allah when they cut the throat of an animal. They cut the throat to completely drain the blood. What does 1Timothy 4:3-5 say about this subject?

> They forbid people to marry and order them to abstain from certain foods, which God created to be received with thanksgiving by those who believe and

who know the truth. For everything God created is good, and nothing is to be rejected if it is received with thanksgiving, because it is consecrated by the word of God and prayer.

Ramadan, the Muslim month of fasting had started. Every evening my wife prepared dates and a sweet yoghurt milk to break the fast. After breaking the fast Muslims usually drink tea and talk together for a long time. A few hours later a large dinner is served. So we adopted this custom in our family. During the whole month of Ramadan we had an average of three people in our house every day, who either broke the fast with us or drank tea and enjoyed the larger dinner. Through this practice we came in contact with dozens of people. At the end of Ramadan we were invited by several of our friends to celebrate the big feast *Eid-ul-Fitr* with them. Through these contacts friendships were developed and some of our friends later accepted Jesus in their lives. Drinking tea, spending time and celebrating the feast with them were ways to establish friendships and to share the good News of Jesus.

Jesus had already clarified this issue in Mark 7:15-19 where we are told explicitly: "In saying this, Jesus declared all foods 'clean'.

Invest much time in relationships

Practicing what we discussed in the preceding sections will almost automatically lead to investing much time in relationships. However, as this is so crucial, we want to underline this principle again: if we do not spend much time with local people, it is impossible to learn their language and culture, to understand them and their context, to build good relationships and.... to be a blessing to them.

The more time we spend with people, the more we will get to know and love them, the more we will also understand their fears, worries and problems and therefore be in a position to really share relevant *Good* News with them. If we are with them often, and enjoying their company, it will also be much easier to actually tell them our story and so, naturally, conversations will sooner or later also turn to spiritual topics, and this will be our natural opportunity to contribute with biblical truths.

An Arab proverb, which is also common in northern Nigeria says, *"Friendship depends on the feet."* In other terms: if I really consider someone as my friend, I will make the effort to visit him. The person I never visit is not important to me. By visiting someone, I honor him. I show him that he is important to me.

Visits are particularly important for people who are facing or experiencing special situations: before or after a long journey, after the birth of a baby, during an illness or after a death in the family. It is in times like these that the extended family and friends will particularly surround the person concerned. If we are present in such circumstances, we show our friend that we are part of his important social circle. Such events also constitute opportunities to give small gifts, or to pray with the person concerned. In some North African culture not to greet an acquaintance who is seriously ill means that one wishes him to die. This shows how important visiting is in most Islamic cultures.

Integrate into society

Integration has different dimensions: People who immigrate for example to Western countries should make an effort to integrate into their new environment, particularly by learning the language and submitting to the law. In the same way a Christian who moves to a specific people group in order to be a blessing should make the effort to be part of their networks. In other words: we need to integrate into society.

Paul was integrated into the social life and the society of those he was seeking to bless with the Good News. He worked with them, lived in their homes, ate with them, spent time with them on the market places and participated in their everyday lives – *he became one of them:*

> One of those listening was a woman named Lydia, a dealer in purple cloth from the city of Thyatira, who was a worshiper of God. The Lord opened her heart to respond to Paul's message. When she and the members of her household were baptized, she invited us to her home. 'If you consider me a believer in the Lord,' she said, 'come and stay at my house.' And she persuaded us. (Acts 16:14-15)

> There he met a Jew named Aquila, a native of Pontus, who had recently come from Italy with his wife Priscilla; because Claudius had ordered all the Jews to leave Rome. Paul went to see them, and because he was a tentmaker as they were, he stayed and worked with them. (Acts 18:2-3)

The natural results of this were in-depth relationships and affection, strong bonds:

> We loved you so much that we were delighted to share with you not only the gospel of God but our lives as well; because you had become so dear to us. Surely you remember, brothers, our toil and hardship; we worked night and day in order not to be a burden to anyone while we preached the gospel of God to you. (1Thess 2:8-9)

It is difficult to accept a new message from a complete stranger. Historically, the Gospel has spread most easily through natural ties of kinship or friendship. You will find more open hearts and ears, if you share the Good News from within a group. Let us rehearse some advice we have learned on how one can integrate into their society:

- o Avoid unnecessary cultural offense
- o Be hospitable and accept their hospitality

- o Invest much time in relationships
- o Do what is exemplary: be loving and friendly
- o Participate in the normal social life of the society (marriages, religious feasts, name giving ceremonies etc.)
- o Assist your acquaintances when they go through difficult times (sickness, death in the family etc.).

Always remember this important principle: *If the group rejects you as the messenger, it will most likely also reject your message. By accepting you as the messenger, it has already taken its first step towards accepting your message!*

Be a tentmaker

The term "tentmaker" is taken from Paul who supported himself by pursuing a secular profession, namely making tents (Acts 18:2-3). This term is used in world missions today to describe someone who has the desire to share the Gospel in a different culture, but works in a secular profession rather than using the title "pastor" or "evangelist". A tentmaker can have much easier access to the local population than someone with the title of a pastor or of a fulltime Christian co-worker.

Biblical Model of Tentmaking

In the New Testament we find two fundamental ways of financing ministry: *tentmaking* (Paul) and *church support* (Peter). Each of them is legitimate in a certain context. Jesus called Peter to leave his fishing activity and to follow him (Luke 5:1-11). After the death of Jesus when he wanted to go back to his previous activity, Jesus renewed Peter's calling (John 21). Years later, Paul wrote that he accepted that Peter and his wife used the support model while undertaking mission journeys (1 Cor. 9:4-5). Paul knew that this was not a problem in the Jewish context, as it was even expected by Jews, but that it could cause alienation in a pioneer context while living among pagans.

Paul, theologian and manufacturer of tents, was the leading pioneer missionary and church planter of the first century. He explained, modeled and energetically defended this type of ministry. Paul knew that he and his team would only be credible and effective as tentmakers. Paul tells us that he preached while he worked during the week, then on the Sabbath, he went into the synagogues to teach the Scriptures (Acts 17:1-3). This is true of his church planting efforts in Thessalonica, Corinth and Ephesus.

- *Thessalonica*

Paul planted a church here on his second mission journey. Reflecting on his time there years later, he wrote:

> Surely you remember, brothers, our toil and hardship; we worked night and day in order not to be a burden to anyone while we preached the gospel of God to you. (1 Thess. 2:9)
>
> Nor did we eat anyone's food without paying for it. On the contrary, we worked day and night, laboring and toiling so that we would not be a burden to any of you. We did this, not because we do not have the right to such help, but in order to make ourselves a model for you to follow. (2 Thess. 3:8-9)

- *Corinth*

When Paul planted the church in Corinth, he worked as a tentmaker alongside Priscilla and Aquila, who had also just arrived in Corinth. (Acts 18:1-3) The tentmaker team worked to earn a living and their ministry among Jews and Greeks went hand in hand with that secular work.

> And because he [Paul] was a tentmaker as they were, he stayed and worked with them. Every Sabbath he reasoned in the synagogue, trying to persuade Jews and Greeks. (Acts 18:3-4)

Years later, Paul defended this strategy in his letter to the church in Corinth. In 1 Corinthians 9:1-18, Paul writes about the legitimate right of servants of God to get support from the church they serve; but in the same breath he defends his strategy to not make use of this right:

> But we did not use this right. On the contrary, we put up with anything rather than hinder the gospel of Christ...In the same way, the Lord has commanded that those who preach the gospel should receive their living from the gospel. But I have not used any of these rights...What then is my reward? Just this: that in preaching the gospel I may offer it free of charge, and so not make use of my rights in preaching it. (1 Cor. 9:12b, 14-15a, 18)

We can conclude that Paul was a tentmaker not for theological, but for strategic and contextual reasons. Later in the chapter we will discuss the reasons for this in greater detail.

- *Ephesus*

The main ministry site of Paul's third journey was Ephesus, which was economically the most important province of the Roman Empire. Paul spent about three years there, and during these three years, the whole Roman province of Asia Minor was reached by the gospel. Even on his third journey, Paul continued tentmaking, although he did receive sporadic financial support from Philippi (2 Cor. 11:9).

Years later, on the occasion of his farewell to the elders of Ephesus, he made the following statements about his ministry among them:

> I have not coveted anyone's silver or gold or clothing. You yourselves know that these hands of mine have supplied my own needs and the needs of my

6. Communicating without Words

companions. In everything I did, I showed you that by this kind of hard work we must help the weak, remembering the words the Lord Jesus himself said: "It is more blessed to give than to receive." (Acts 20:33-35)

Paul applied the tentmaker model, and God blessed his secular activity to such an extent that through his work he was able to not only sustain his own living but also that of his team. He was also able to support "the weak". The tentmaker model in church planting was a non-negotiable for Paul, a core principle that he did not allow to be questioned. When his apostolic ministry was in the crossfire of critics in Corinth because he worked with his hands, he once more defended vehemently this very strategy:

> Was it a sin for me to lower myself in order to elevate you by preaching the gospel of God free of charge? I robbed other churches by receiving support from them so as to serve you. And when I was with you and needed something, I was not a burden for anyone, for the brothers who came from Macedonia supplied what I needed. I have kept myself from being a burden to you in any way, and will continue to do so. As sure as the truth of Christ is in me, nobody in the regions of Achaia will stop this boasting of mine. (2 Cor. 11:7-10)

Paul humbled himself through his manual labor, so that he would burden no one. He may have received occasional help from Philippi, the only church that financially supported him, but he didn't ask for it (Phil. 4:17) and he consistently earned his living through manual labor (2 Cor. 12:14). Here is what he wrote to the Philippians:

> You Philippians know very well that when I left Macedonia in the early days of preaching the Good News, you were the only church to help me; you were the only ones who shared my profits and losses. More than once when I needed help in Thessalonica, you sent it to me. (Phil. 4:15-16, GNB, italics added)

We see that Paul vehemently defended his use of the tentmaker model on several occasions. He worked as a tentmaker because of a deep conviction and strategic principles, not only when church support was not available. Furthermore, Paul urged others to follow this example:

> We did this, not because we do not have the right to such help, but in order to make ourselves a model for you to follow. For even when we were with you, we gave you this rule: "If a man will not work, he shall not eat." (2 Thess. 3:9-10)

Therefore we see that tentmaking was not only the biblical model of the church planting pioneers, but also carried a strategic mandate.

Strategic Mandate

- *Tentmakers are better accepted and have more credibility.*

Paul says that he worked as a tentmaker that he might not hinder the gospel:

> If others have this right of support from you, shouldn't we have it all the more? *But we did not use this right.* On the contrary, we put up with anything rather than hinder the gospel of Christ. (1Cor. 9:12, italics added)

Paul rejects financial support not for theological reasons, but for strategic reasons. He does not want to hinder the gospel; rather, he wants to be credible. If the messenger is not credible, it is almost impossible to make his message credible. Before an audience accepts the message, it must accept the messenger.

- *Tentmakers have a natural bridge to the local population.*

In many cases, fully supported co-workers have to earn the right of access into the local population. They have to look out for opportunities to meet people. Maybe they start visiting people in their homes, which in the eyes of the local population is seen as artificial, abnormal, and unnatural. Tentmakers, on the other hand, live in the midst of the society. Through their secular job they are naturally connected to dozens, even hundreds of people, and through these natural relationships they can build bridges to extended families without raising suspicion, and naturally share the gospel.

> A tentmaker working as a gardener testified: "I find the best opportunities for spreading the gospel seed right in the garden, under a mango tree, when we gardeners all rest together after work." He worked and sweat with the other men of the village to feed their families, and when they rested together under a mango tree he, *being one of them,* was able to share the message. His agricultural work was the bridge, through which he became, in a natural way, a blessing to the village.

> Another messenger, working as an agriculturalist-tentmaker in a rural area, introduced several new planting methods. He put a great deal of effort into it and cultivated the largest field in the village. Accordingly, his harvest was plenty. One day the village chief told me: "If this man stays in our village, we will never be hungry again." Because of this great witness through his tentmaker work, the man was accepted by the local population – and on that foundation, he was able to share the Gospel in a credible way. He even got permission to announce the Good New publicly during market days.

- *Tentmakers identify themselves with the local population.*

Paul was a highly qualified theologian and was therefore able to identify with the Jewish scholars in the Synagogues and the Greek philosophers. But how was he going to share with the ordinary people? Only by living and working like them, by placing himself on their level, by identifying with them – by following the example of Jesus in Philippians 2:5-11.

> He was able to say: "We work hard with our own hands" (1Cor 4:12a).

He worked hard with his own hands like the people he wanted to reach; he was therefore respected by them and was able to reach the many ordinary folk.

6. Communicating without Words

- *Tentmakers proclaim the gospel by doing secular work under the power of the Holy Spirit.*

Tentmakers share the gospel not only in words, but also in deed. They stand in the midst of life, through an authentic Biblical lifestyle. They demonstrate without words that the gospel is also relevant in the storms of daily life. They *are* the gospel through their everyday life:

- A businesswoman when she trades with fair prices, tells the truth, and is generous.
- A judge when he does not accept bribes and always judges by the law.
- A teacher when she teaches with enthusiasm and dedication, and always gives fair grades.
- A farmer when he sows in his fields with prayer and faith in the Creator.
- A nurse or doctor when they tend to their patients with love and care, amplifying their work with prayer, possibly for healing as prompted by the Holy Spirit.

The performance of secular work under the power of the Holy Spirit is Good News without words and paves the way for the witness with words.

- *Tentmakers model a biblical lifestyle for new believers.*

New believers do not have examples of authentic followers of Jesus. They cannot know how biblical ethics can be evidenced in their society and culture. Paul demonstrated biblical living because no one in the region had ever seen a true believer. He lived a holy life in the same immoral, idolatrous, cesspool society where he expected new believers to live holy lives. Paul also modeled a Biblical work ethic in this culture where indolence and thievery were the norm. Paul says much in his brief letters about work, because without strong work ethic, there could not be godly followers of Jesus, healthy families, independent faith communities – nor productive societies.

Believers must learn how to live out their new faith within their society. Tentmakers therefore become models of how to live that life. A fully supported co-worker cannot be as effective of a role model for them in this way.

- *Tentmakers are at least partly financially autonomous.*

Most churches do not have enough in their budgets to support full time co-workers for ministry among people of other cultures. Tentmakers are inexpensive because they are partially or completely self-supported. Tentmaking makes it possible for all churches to release more co-workers for that type of work.

- *Tentmakers model strategies for support and ministry to future leaders.*

Typically, house fellowships are led by heads of households who work in a secular job to feed their families and welcome the fellowship into their home. Such small house fellowships or cell groups do not have the financial means to employ a full-time pastor. If the messengers among them demonstrate the tentmaker model, it will seem normal to the leaders to serve their house fellowships as tentmakers, too.

It is only when a network of a few house fellowships is established that the need for a full-time shepherd will appear, but at that point the network will be financially strong enough to finance such a coworker without outside help.

- *Tentmakers can be multiplied easily.*

If we only rely on full-time and academically trained co-workers, we will never reach the goal of blessing all peoples. Not every follower of Jesus is called to study at a seminary – but every follower of Jesus is called to spread the Good News in and through his daily life. Every mature follower of Jesus working in a secular job and living under the guidance of the Holy Spirit qualifies to serve as a tentmaker.

- *Tentmakers have access to so-called "closed countries".*

In many countries, it is not possible to officially obtain visas for fulltime Christian co-workers: fully supported "professional Christians" do not have access to many people groups because the governments of these countries will not grant them visas. Tentmakers, on the other hand, can obtain their visa and residence permit through their professional qualifications. Therefore, they are also able to live and minister in these so-called "closed countries." We prefer to call this category of countries "Creative Access Countries" – because no countries are closed for God. Since access into many countries today is only possible through tentmaking, it is virtually impossible to fulfill our mandate of blessing all peoples without implementing this approach.

- *Tentmakers are also full-time.*

A tentmaker ministers full-time while being a full-time employee. Their tentmaker job is the God-given context in which they constantly share the Good News. Because tentmakers are always with the people that they want to reach, they can always share – through words and actions!

Paul emphasizes the importance of *"workplace evangelism"*: He modeled and taught workplace evangelism because most people spent most of their time at work. Sharing the Good News in the marketplace was the best way to infiltrate society, because it was the place where people of every social level rubbed shoulders. In his letters, he described this strategy to believers:

6. Communicating without Words

> Be wise in the way you act towards outsiders; make the most of every opportunity. Let your conversation be always full of grace, seasoned with salt, so that you may know how to answer everyone. (Col 4:5-6)

The Greek word for 'time' that Paul uses here is "*kairos*" – God's time, a special opportunity. In their daily contact with unbelievers, tentmakers should listen for the Holy Spirit, so that in a God-given moment they can give a loving ("full of grace") and challenging ("with a pinch of salt") word. According to this passage in Colossians, workplace evangelism consists of four fundamental elements (compare also with Eph 6:5-8 and Col 4:5-6):

- Personal integrity ("Be wise")
- Commitment to quality work, good use of time ("make the most of every opportunity")
- Loving, gentle relationships ("full of grace")
- Short, fitting, evangelistic comments at the right time ("seasoned with salt")

The New Testament teaching about evangelism addresses lifestyle much more than techniques. *Our whole life is worship, and our whole life is evangelism.* The tentmaker does not go out to share Good News – he himself as a person is Good News and a fragrance that spreads the sweet smell of Christ.

- *Tentmakers can be extremely efficient.*

You might wonder whether tentmakers with their demanding job requirements can be as efficient as full-time co-workers. Let us again listen to Paul who after twenty years of ministry as a tentmaker writes this to the Romans:

> So from Jerusalem all the way round to Illyricum, I have fully proclaimed the gospel of Christ… But now that there is no more place for me to work in these regions… (Rom 15:19b-23a)

Paul had completed his work in six Roman provinces – in the whole southern, Greek-speaking Mediterranean area – and had planted local faith communities everywhere with just a handful of outside coworkers and with little financial support. Paul's tentmaker job did not hinder him from being efficient. On the contrary, his example challenged believers and emerging leaders to follow him and share the Good News while working as tentmakers. As well, we should remember that very few tentmakers work full-time in a secular job. Most of them carry out a part-time activity, which allows them to make initial contacts and share the gospel while working in the secular job, and teach new believers in their spare time.

Biblical Strategy	Tentmakers follow the biblical model of the pioneering church planters
Credibility	Tentmakers are accepted and credible in the eyes of the local population
Natural Bridge	Tentmakers have a natural bridge to the local population through their secular job
Identification	Tentmakers identify themselves with the local population.
Comprehensive Proclamation	Tentmakers proclaim the gospel through spirit-filled secular work.
Model for New Believers	Tentmakers model a Christian lifestyle for new believers.
No Financial Dependency	Tentmakers are at least partly financially autonomous.
Model for Future Leaders	Tentmakers model strategies for support and ministry to future church leaders.
Multiplication	Tentmakers can be multiplied easily.
Unlimited Access	Tentmakers have access to so-called "closed countries."
Integrated Work and Ministry	Tentmakers are full-time missionaries in a work context.
Efficiency	Tentmakers are just as efficient as fully supported, full-time missionaries.

Table 4: Summary of the Tentmaker Strategy

Be authentic and credible

If you live your faith in an authentic and credible way, two important things will happen: God will use you to bring blessing to other people, and you will find open ears and hearts.

We can compare our life to a cup that God uses to bring blessing to all cultures. No one is happy if someone gives him a drink in a dirty cup. We do not drink from a dirty cup because we can catch all sorts of diseases. The Bible says:

> If a man cleanses himself from the latter, he will be an instrument for noble purposes, made holy, useful to the Master and prepared to do any good work. (2Tim 2:.21)

God wants to offer all peoples clean water in a clean cup. Even if you are very thirsty, you do not want to have a drink if the cup is dirty. In the same way, even if unbelievers want to know more about Jesus, it will be hard for them to listen if our lives are not authentic and transparent. The message of the gospel is like cool, pure water for a thirsty person – however, if we do not present it clean, e.g. authentic and credible, no-one is keen to "drink" it. We are not perfect. We will get it wrong, particularly as tentmakers, in the daily life of the secular world and also in our opening our homes to them. How should we handle our failures?

- Confess our sins to God
- Ask for forgiveness from your friends and repair the damage as much as possible
- Do everything to follow the example of the Apostle Paul who had a pure conscience before God and men:

> So I strive always to keep my conscience clear before God and man. (Acts 24.16)

Make a difference by acts of love

> For we do not preach ourselves, but Jesus Christ as Lord, and ourselves as your servants for Jesus' sake. (2Cor 4:5)

This is an important verse for this first phase of our communication cycle: *we make ourselves their servants for Jesus' sake*. When we start to intentionally serve other people, they will wonder why we are doing this. And just this question will open the door for you to share in a non-aggressive way your love for Jesus which really is the root of your love for them.

> In one country in North Africa, followers of Jesus visited a strong Islamic town for one week. Instead of immediately sharing the Gospel with words, they prayed for the first two days. After this, they cleaned all of the public places of the town (market, hospital etc.) for two days. This town had never been clean like it was during those days. The local people were so surprised that they asked questions: "Why are you doing this?" This question opened wide the door to share the Good News with words.

In the past, the contact between Muslims and Christians has too often been characterized by hot discussions, aggressive debates and attacking terminology. In most cases, this approach had led to a dead end and did certainly not bring a blessing to the Muslims. It seems obvious: *They might always question our arguments, but they will not question our acts of service done in real love.* This basic attitude of loving service was also Jesus' motivation. After washing his disciples' feet, he asks them to follow this example:

> I have set you an example that you should do as I have done for you. (Jn 13:15)

And Paul describes in Phil. 2:7, how Jesus made himself a volunteer slave of all men:

> ...but made himself nothing, taking the very nature of a servant, being made in human likeness. (Phil 2:7)

We must seize every possibility to do little acts of love in everyday life. Such a lifestyle will speak much louder than any hot discussion or verbal argument. Love is the Christian's supreme apologetic (apologetic = defense of our faith)! *One of the main attributes of God is love, so only a loving witness is God-glorifying.*

> This love can be shown in countless ways: sometimes a friendly smile at the right time can make a difference; or visiting an old or sick person; or a phone call, a short visit; or a practical help, when moving or after an accident; sometimes showing love and kindness to children can be the key to their parents' heart; or showing real interest in the well-being of a neighbor or a colleague at the work place.

If we really have love in our hearts, we will find 1001 ways a day to show this love through tangible deeds and kind words

7
Communicating with Words

Introduction

We now arrive at the second phase of our cycle: the verbal communication. It is important to note that Chapter Seven builds on Chapter Six. Without a powerful and genuine communication without words, the communication with words will most likely not be credible or effective. *Our verbal communication builds on our non-verbal communication.*

To return to our comparison with construction work: this second phase would correspond to the walls. If we stop working when the foundation is complete, that would be pointless. But if we build the walls without a good foundation, that would also be pointless. In our work, therefore, we construct a good foundation (first phase), but we never stop there. In other words: the time must come when we also open our mouth in order to share the Good News and to extend God's blessing to them through words, too. Ultimately, faith comes from hearing.

Let us be aware that we are meeting individuals and not a religion. They are people like us, with questions, problems, needs and hopes; and we can assume that God has given us something to bless them and to draw them closer to the One who is able to really meet their deepest needs.

Choose an appropriate time and place

Every society and culture has appropriate times and places for certain things or events. If we choose an inappropriate moment to speak about an important matter, the person will not listen to us. Not because of the subject, but because of the inappropriate time. Think about the example of the child who wants to speak to his father who in the middle of selling something in his shop. Even though he loves his child, the father will not listen to him because he is too busy at that precise moment. These times and places differ from one society to the other; therefore, we must do some research and identify these times.

A look at Jesus' ministry shows that he was very flexible and adapted his program to the availability and needs of the people: Jesus welcomed Nicodemus alone at his home at night (Jn 3); he met the Samaritan woman alone at the well at noon (Jn 4); he joined two men on a walk late afternoon on the way to Emmaus (Lk 24:13-15, 27). These were three very different kinds of people and three very different places and times – but Jesus always pursued the same goal: To meet those people's needs and to bless them with the communication of the Good News.

Jesus chose the times when they were available and ready to listen. In the case of the two men on the road to Emmaus, they were already in the middle of a discussion. Jesus simply joined them and took part in their conversation.

It is important to note that times and places should suit the local people, not us. Many non-Western cultures have a very different rhythm or daily schedule. Sometimes, social times take place late evening or even at night. The day might start later in the morning. Co-workers from Western cultures with their rigid schedules must learn a big deal of flexibility to adapt their rhythm. Here again an example of Jesus' ministry:

> Then, because so many people were coming and going that they did not even have a chance to eat, he said to them, 'Come with me by yourselves to a quiet place and get some rest. So they went away by themselves in a boat to a solitary place. But many who saw them leaving recognized them and ran on foot from all the towns and got there ahead of them. When Jesus landed and saw a large crowd, he had compassion on them, because they were like sheep without a shepherd. So he began teaching them many things. (Mk 6:31-34)

The time did not suit Jesus at all because he had planned to have a rest. However, the crowd wanted to listen to him. Therefore Jesus began to teach. He was not thinking about his own concerns. He was thinking first and foremost about others.

Do not forget that people might not always be open to your message. If they are available to listen today, you should not miss this opportunity. For who guarantees that they will still listen to you when it will be suitable to you? – Jesus seized every opportunity, whenever people were open to listen, to share something about God's Kingdom.

Create a suitable framework

Isn't it much easier to listen to someone when we feel totally at ease? We listen more easily in a relaxed atmosphere, without stress and in a pleasant place. Create a setting that will facilitate good communication. Of course, this framework changes from culture to culture. You will therefore have to observe first what is happening, so that you can adapt appropriately to their behavior pattern.

Here is an example for a rather Arab-oriental society:

- *Arabs love tea:* (in many Arab cultures it would be unthinkable to have a meaningful conversation with a friend without a glass of tea). A meal also can contribute a lot to create a relaxed atmosphere.

- *Arabs value relationships:* it is therefore advisable to create good relationships with them and then naturally share seeds of the Gospel with them on the basis of that relationship.

- *Arabs trust in their families and friends:* in view of the later house fellowships of believers, it is ideal when the Good News is shared from the start in the trusted frame of family and friends. In many contexts, it is less advisable to organize public mass events. A smaller, trusted, relational setting is most appropriate.

- *Arabs defend their honor:* A Muslim might take a risk when he asks spiritual questions or listens to the Good News. Respect this reality and make sure that he is really ready to speak with you about spiritual things. You might possibly have to identify a discreet place, so that you will not be disturbed during your conversation and without feeling threatened by anyone. In any case, he will always defend his honor and the honor of his people

Many Muslim fathers can be compared to Nicodemus. Jesus did not condemn Nicodemus because he came to see him at night at a very discreet place. He didn't tell him to come publically forward the next day in the Synagogue if he had any questions to ask him. Jesus knew how risky it could possibly be for Nicodemus to come to him in public. Instead of criticizing him, he made the most of the occasion to share Good News with Nicodemus, and he did this in a way that was most suitable, in which he could relax and feel totally at ease. If Jesus had preached the same message to the same Nicodemus in public, he would not have been able to listen to him.

Find persons of peace – bless whole families

As we already saw in our introduction: it is God's plan and intention to bless all families on earth through the Good News. *Oikos* is the Greek term for "household", "family". When we study the Gospels and the book of Acts, we see that both Jesus and his disciples aimed at blessing the whole *oikos*, whole families. They followed already existing family ties and other natural social networks. They were the most normal channel for the Gospel to spread into new areas. In order to bless all families on earth, Jesus recommended to his disciples a specific strategy: in all new areas, they should first identify a person of peace. They should then stay in his house, eat and drink with him, bless him in prayer and announce to him and his *oikos* the arrival and the blessings of the Kingdom of God (cp. Luke 10 : 1-11; Mt. 10 : 5-14). The house of the man of peace will then become the base for a new house fellowship, particularly if the members of his family and social network become followers of Jesus at the same time with him, as in the example of Cornelius in Acts 10.

Here is a summary of Jesus' recommendations for co-workers:
- Based on divine promises, they have a strong vision for an abundant spiritual harvest (Lk 10:2)
- They water their efforts with lots of prayer (Lk 10:2)
- They go under a divine mandate (Mat 10:5-6)
- They seek and identify a person of peace, and when they have found her, they concentrate on this person (Mat 10:11)
- They bring "the Shalom of God" (Luke 10:5). Whoever accepts this divine Shalom is a person of peace.
- They have fellowship with this person of peace, spend lots of time with her and the entire *oikos*, eat and drink with them (Lk 10:7-8)
- They bring the physical blessings of the Kingdom to the *oikos*: they pray for the sick and other needs of the family (Lk 10:10)
- They announce the blessings of the Kingdom with the entire *oikos* (Lk 10:10)
- If the reaction is negative, they leave this house and go on to look for another person of peace (Lk 10:11).

Here some characteristics of a person of peace:
- She opens her house to the messenger and welcomes him (Lk 10:5)
- She is open to receive the blessings of the messenger and listens to him (Lk 10:6)
- She has influence on an entire *oikos* (Mat 10:13)
- She is hospitable (Lk 10:7).

Western cultures are characterized by an extreme individualism. However, in most non-western cultures, important decisions are made by consensus, after extended discussion with the family and its social network.

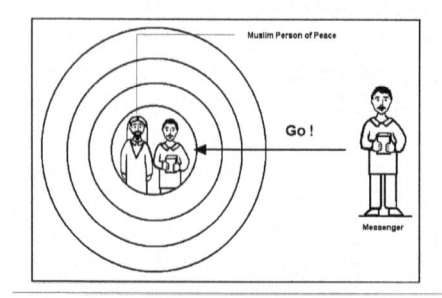

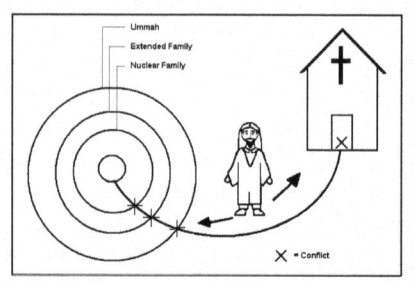

Figure 5: Person of Peace Strategy: "Go" versus "Come"

7. Communicating without Words 65

Figure 5 illustrates the person of peace strategy: Jesus does not tell us to call people into our church buildings. *Instead of us telling persons of peace to come to our church, Jesus tells us to go into their communities.* Of course it is much easier for us to simply ask people to join us in our church. However, this methodology creates lots of unnecessary conflict for the Muslim, first with his Ummah (which does no longer consider him as belonging to them), but often also with the church (where his culture does not fit). Many Muslims like Jesus, but they do not like our way of doing church. They want to follow him, but they also want to remain part of their community. The person of peace approach has a solution for this problem, as it does not condition the acceptance of Jesus as Savior to the adherence of a foreign church form and culture. When working with Muslims, we should bring them *"Jesus plus nothing"*!

The New Testament mentions several persons of peace by their names: Cornelius (Acts 10), Lydia (Acts 16:11-15), the jailor (Acts 16:25-40), Aquila und Priscilla (Acts 18:1-4; Rom 16:3-5), Crispus (Acts 18:7-8), Stephanus (1Cor 1:16), Archippus (Phl 1:2), Publius (Acts 28:7-10), and others.

The Cornelius story helps us to better understand some more of the underlying principles (Acts 10):

- Prayer is the starting point: the messenger, Peter, as well as the man of peace, Cornelius, are praying; Cornelius is seeking (2, 9)
- God sends a vision to both Peter and Cornelius; whereas Cornelius only needs one vision to obey, Peter needs three times the same vision until he reluctantly agrees to obey.....
- God helps Peter to overcome cultural barriers and obstacles (15)
- Despite some initial reservations and fears, Peter is willing to go with radical obedience (20, 21, 23)
- Peter works in a team (23)
- Peter finds the man of peace and stays in his house (25)
- Peter shares Good News in the home of the man of peace (24)
- Cornelius is not alone; rather, he had already gathered, prepared and invited his entire social network (family, neighbors, friends) to listen to the message of the Gospel (24, 27)
- Peter does not try to set up any secret meetings with Cornelius; rather, he shares Good News in this semi-public setting of trusted family members and friends (24, 27)
- Peter shares the fundamental truths of the Gospel (38-43)
- The real messenger is the Holy Spirit: he convicts the listeners (44)

- Peter spends enough time with this *oikos* to teach and edify (48)
- The result of this effort was a new house fellowship in Caesarea.

In family oriented cultures it is best to share Good News in a family oriented way. Past strategies have encouraged messengers to concentrate on individuals. The result of this was that new believers were often isolated or persecuted by their families, because instead of being viewed by the family as a blessing, the Gospel was viewed as something that tore families apart. It is therefore much more effective to include entire families from the start. This might have as a consequence that the whole process slows down; however, it follows much more the divine mandate of blessing all families on earth, because the family structure is respected and families will not be torn apart.

We would therefore encourage you to identify men and women of peace. When you have found them, encourage them to also include their social network (nuclear and extended family, neighbors and friends).

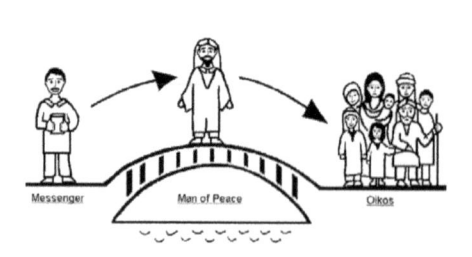

Then plan to implant Good News into this *oikos* in a non-aggressive way. When you do, use the various principles that we introduced in this chapter. As the New Testament examples show, the *oikos* of the person of peace can naturally become the starting point for a new fellowship of believers – in his home.

Figure 6: The person of peace

Pray *with* Muslims and pray *for* their needs

It is significant to note that in the above mentioned "person of peace" strategy, Jesus advices his disciples to first heal the sick and then only verbally share the Kingdom of God. So often we reverse the order. We start to verbally share theological truth with a Muslim only to get stuck in endless arguments. If they first experience the power of God in their lives through prayer (blessing, healing, deliverance) the theological discussion will become much easier. In Muslim context, therefore, start at the experiential (God's power) rather than at the intellectual level (theological arguments).

One of the best ways to bless Muslims is prayer for them and their needs. If you are from a Western background, this might surprise you. However, particularly co-workers in an Asian or African context will quickly notice how

7. Communicating without Words

natural the factor "God" flows into daily life. Spontaneous prayer in tough situations such as accidents, loss, pain, conflicts, family problems and others is just natural. When praying for Muslims, be aware of the following:

- The Muslim already knows from the Qur'an that Jesus has the power to heal the sick. Therefore, in most cases, a prayer in the name of Jesus is acceptable to him. It is more appropriate to pray in Jesus name to God the Creator than to address the prayer directly to Jesus.

- Use titles for Jesus that are known and acceptable to Muslims (e.g. "Isa al-Masih")

- Most Muslims only know the ritual prayer in Arabic. In many non-Arab contexts, this fact leaves a big vacuum, as many do not really understand what they are praying. To have a personal relationship with God is unthinkable for most Muslims. It will therefore be most surprising to him when you speak directly with God in prayer, in your mother tongue and with personal words. He will be amazed about your direct access to God the Father, as a child to his father. Therefore, even if there was no direct response to your prayer, just the fact of a most personal prayer to a personal God is a very strong message for any Muslim.

- According to the situation, the time of prayer could be introduced by a reading of the Bible. For example, if you are praying for a sick person, you could first of all read or tell the story of a healing by Jesus in the *Injil* and then perhaps even leave him an *Injil*.

Praying for the sick or generally for the direct intervention of God in specific situations is biblical:

> Everyone was filled with awe, and many wonders and miraculous signs were done by the apostles. (Acts 2:43)

> Then Peter said, 'Silver or gold I do not have, but what I have I give you. In the name of Jesus Christ of Nazareth, walk. (Acts 3:6)

> When the crowds heard Philip and saw the miraculous signs he did, they all paid attention to what he said. (Acts 8:6)

> At that, the man jumped up and began to walk. (Acts 14:10)

> My message and my preaching were not with wise and persuasive words, but with a demonstration of the Spirit's power... (1Cor 2:4)

Prayer for a person in need is always an expression of our love. This love will touch him, even if there was no direct answer to this prayer. We cannot force God to answer our prayers.

Particularly in a Popular Islamic context, this type of intercession is essential. These Muslims are always looking for more *Baraka*, blessing, and seek it at all possible places through all possible means. When they contact a local Sheikh to get more *Baraka*, they have to pay for it or to offer sacrifices. An authentic follower of Jesus, who simply – and of course free of charge – prays in the name of *Isa al- Masih*, will touch them.

Build on the truth which they already know

There are fragments of truth in all cultures and religions – possibly not the whole truth, but very precious aspects or elements of truth. *All truth is God's truth:* God Himself put it in their hearts (Rom 2:15). We should identify it and build on it. Paul worked according to this principle:

> God did this so that men would seek him and perhaps reach out for him and find him, though he is not far from each one of us. 'For in him we live and move and have our being.' As some of your own poets have said, 'We are his offspring.' (Acts 17:27-28)

The Greeks liked poetry and poets. Paul listened to them and simply repeated what these poets had said. After this the people enjoyed listening to what Paul had to say to them. Athens was a city full of heresies, idols and sin. Paul had many reasons to criticize and confront the Greeks. However, he chose another path, that of filtering out what was good among them and then building on this and leading them a step further: to the knowledge that Jesus is the Messiah and the Judge of the whole world (Acts 17:31). Therefore the principle is the following:

- Identify the truths which already exist in the Islamic teaching
- Identify and transmit what they still need

We have already spoken about the importance of listening to them before speaking ourselves. It is only when we know their teaching that we can implement the principles of this section.

If we study more of the Qur'an, we will discover that in fact the content of the two books, the Bible and the Qur'an, resemble each other in some ways. There are also quite a few differences. We should be aware of the similarities as well as of the differences. Then we should ask ourselves: Where should we start our communication? Should we start with things on which we agree or with things on which we disagree? – Each similarity, each agreement, each piece of common truth can be a bridge on which we can walk a step further towards a Muslim. Each piece of truth in their teaching can be an additional stone on which we can build more truth. Here a few examples for such stones. They can serve us as bridges:

7. Communicating without Words

- *Some teaching about God*

There is only one God, he is the Creator, he is without sin, etc. The "99 beautiful names of Allah" (Al-Asma Al-Husna) play a prominent role in the lives of many Muslims (reciting these with the help of a tasbih); each of them has a Biblical parallel reference (see Encountering the World of Islam, pages 469-471).

- *Some of the prophets*

Many Biblical "prophets" are also known in the Qur'an: Adam, Noah, Abraham, Isaac, Jacob, Joseph, Moses, Aaron, David, Job, Jonah, John and many others. The Qur'an mentions 25 prophets by name; 22 of them are also mentioned in the Bible.

- *The books of the prophets*

Muslims believe that God gave the Taurat to Moses, the Zabur to David, and the Injil to Jesus. These three books correspond to the Pentateuch, the Psalms and the Gospels. Every Muslim must believe that these books constitute the revelation of God. In these books, we have many things in common, e.g. the story of creation or the story of the birth of Jesus.

- *Some teachings about Jesus*

All Muslims honor Jesus and consider him a great prophet. He is mentioned in 15 Suras and 93 verses. His main names are Isa (25x), Isa Ibn Maryam (23x) and Isa al Masih (11x). No other prophet is referred to in the Qur'an as often as Jesus is.

Many Islamic teachings about Jesus correspond to Biblical teachings, such as:

- o His unique origin: Muslims believe that Jesus came directly from God
- o His unique birth. Muslims believe that Jesus was born from a virgin. In the Qur'an, Jesus is not called "Isa Ibn Yousouf" (Jesus son of Joseph), but rather "Isa Ibn Meryam" (Jesus son of Mary). Muslims believe that Jesus did not have a human father (Sura 3:45-47, compare with Mt 1:23).
- o His unique miracles: In the Qur'an, Jesus raises the dead, heals the sick, opens the eyes of the blind (Sura 3:49; 5:110).
- o His unique titles: Messiah, spirit of God, Word of God, Word of truth (and many more, see appendix for a complete presentation of the Jesus titles in the Qur'an).
- o His innocence: In the Qur'an, Jesus is called the pure (holy, innocent) (Sura 19:19).

- His unique current position: According to the Qur'an, Allah raised Jesus to himself where he currently is (Sura 3:55)
- His return: Muslims believe that Jesus will come back to earth in the end-time. So strictly speaking, not Muhammad, but rather Jesus is the last prophet (43:61).

Not just in the Bible, but even according to Islamic teaching, there is no other person or even prophet as unique and supernatural as Jesus. Of course, other prophets healed the sick (Elisha), came directly from God (Adam) or rose directly to God (Elijah), but only in the person of Jesus are the above mentioned things combined – and Muslims even believe that he is alive today! Therefore, even without opening your Bible, you can share with a Muslim a lot of Biblical teaching about Jesus simply by highlighting what he already believes! Then, encourage him to discover more about this unique prophet by reading himself the Injil.

- *Belief in demons and angels*

Muslims believe in demons and angels. They believe that angels are messengers of God who sometimes appear to men to give them a message from God.

- *The day of final judgment*

Every Muslim knows that there will be a day when God judges the living and the dead. The Day of Judgment is one of the two great themes of the Qur'an and of Islamic tradition.

- *Heaven and hell*

Even though the Muslim's ideas concerning these places are different from the Biblical teaching, he knows that these places exist. He knows that hell is a bad place and he will do anything to enter heaven. Here are some examples of how to put this principle into practice:

- Telling stories from the Old Testament or reading together in the Old Testament as a preparation for the New Testament teaching. Choose particularly stories about prophets that are also mentioned in the Qur'an.
- You can ask a Muslim to tell you what the Qur'an says about the birth of Jesus. You listen to him without argument or discussion. When he has finished, you ask him if he wants to know what the Injil says about it. Since you have listened until he has finished, he will also listen to you. Then you read Luke 1 with him, emphasizing the points which you have in common (there are quite a few!). Then show him Mt 1:21, which explains why Jesus was born in a particular way: to save men from their sins.

- *Isa al-Masih*, Jesus the Messiah, is a title often used in the Qur'an for Jesus (11x). You can ask a Muslim to tell you what he understands by this title. Listen to him attentively. Then tell him what it means in the Bible: the one, who is anointed, set apart for God to carry out a special task: to heal the sick, to set free the oppressed and to save sinners.

Qur'an verses or stories are bridges that can lead a Muslim to seek for more truth in God's Word. A bridge is never a goal in itself; it is rather a means to get to a new place. We can build on the points we have in common in order to lead the person towards the Bible where he will find the whole truth. The points in common are not an aim in themselves. Rather they are bridges which lead us to the aim. For obvious reasons you should have read through the whole Qur'an first and have a good grasp of its main tenets, before stepping out on such a "bridge". Many an unprepared witness has lost balance and found himself in "deep water" by referring to what he did not know.

In the Appendixes, you will find additional suggestions on how the Qur'an can be used in evangelism.

Do not provoke people, but rather avoid disputes

Proverbs gives us the following advice:

> A gentle answer turns away wrath, but a harsh word stirs up anger. (Prov 15:1)

As bearers of blessing, we are not called to provoke others or to seek quarrels; rather, we should be peacemakers.

How can we avoid quarrels and provocation?

- *Don't begin your conversation with words which will anger your listener*

Quarrels will never lead to anything good. This is particularly the case in oriental, but also in African cultures where maintaining one's honor is viewed as much more important than mere knowledge. In such a context, maintaining a good relationship and mutual respect may be more important than a "verbal triumph". Yes, we must say the truth, even if it challenges, but we must not necessarily begin with the aspects of truth that we know will provoke. There is a right way, a right time and a right place to say the full truth. Examples for provoking words are the divine title for Jesus or offensive titles for their prophet. We should be wise by using other, equally biblical terms for Jesus such as "Jesus the Messiah" or "Jesus, the Son of Mary". We can show respect to their prophet, because his teaching contains also elements of truth. Did you actually know that the two leading elements in his teaching were "there is only one God" and "there will be a final judgment day"? Are these two elements not also biblical?

- *Don't seek to speak in the places where quarrels often take place*

In many non-western cultures, examples for such places are the market, public places or the mosque. A better approach would be to begin by sharing Good News without words and then implementing the principles of this chapter. If a difficult situation arises in spite of all your precautions, you should follow the teaching of Paul:

> Don't have anything to do with foolish and stupid arguments, because you know that they produce quarrels. And the Lord's servant must not quarrel; instead, he must be kind to everyone, able to teach, not resentful. Those who oppose him he must gently instruct, in the hope that God will grant them repentance leading them to a knowledge of the truth... (2 Tim 2:23-25).

- Remember that a bearer of blessing is not called to quarrel. If the other person starts to quarrel, it is better to always respond with gentleness, kindness, love and patience.
- Never get angry or annoyed.
- If the discussion becomes aggressive or confrontational, orientate the subject differently or emphasize a point which unites you, on which you can both agree.
- You might also quote some verses from the Qur'an which encourage Muslims to love and respect true Christians, for example Surah 5:82 or Surah 10:94.
- If it is necessary, break off the conversation. Even Jesus did not enter all conversations. Neither did he answer to all the questions he was asked. Sometimes his answers were intentionally vague (in front of Pilate: "You have said it"); sometimes he did not reply at all (in front of Herod), sometimes he proclaimed everything in public (Sermon on the Mount). Be wise, but at the same time avoid being afraid and don't forget that *it is easy to win a hot debate while losing the person.*

Teach chronologically

A main problem between the Qur'an and the Bible is that they use the same vocabulary, but mean different concepts with the same words. Their terms might be the same, but the contents, the concepts and definitions might be quite different.

When we speak with Muslims, misunderstandings are therefore almost unavoidable. Even on the level of the foundational religious terms, the corresponding contents are not the same. The following table summarizes some of these terms:

7. Communicating without Words

Concept	Bible	Muslim Worldview
The love and faithfulness of God	God loves sinners unconditionally; he is 100% faithful to his Word	God loves the one who loves him; God loves his followers and slaves but hates his enemies. He is too great to be tied to his own Word
Man	Evil, sinner, lost without hope, separated from God, has need of a Savior	Good, but weak; is not separated from God, does not need a Savior; needs only guidance
Holiness	Interior, right down to motivations, desires and thoughts of the heart, cf. Sermon on the Mount	Exterior; Purification possible through receiving a ritual bath (Ghusl (ritual bath) and ritual washing (wudu-ablution).
Sin	Man sins because he is evil; he is a sinner and he wants to sin; he is responsible.	Predestination; man sins because God created him weak; every good or evil action is the result of God's predestination
Prayer	Like a child who speaks with his father, having fellowship with the father because of a relationship of love; in any language	Like a slave, who is submitted to his master, it is a relationship of the slave to his master; only acceptable in Arabic and if rituals are performed correctly; fellowship with God is not possible.
The solution	Jesus Christ, the atoning sacrifice for our sins	Following the right religion, that is Islam
Salvation	By faith in Jesus Christ who died for our sins, it is not by works, but by grace; assurance of salvation	By performing exterior rituals (5 pillars); through works, concept of scales; no assurance of salvation (*Insha'Allah* = if God wills…); God has already consigned to hell whomever he wanted; fate cannot be changed – everything is already written.
Paradise	A beautiful place; to be in the presence of God, praise and worship, spiritual	A beautiful place; its chief pleasures are food and sex (beautiful virgins); no fellowship with God; sensual
Hell	Hell Eternal separation from God, eternal conscious suffering	Separation from God; not eternal for Muslims; Popular: suffering can be shortened by the prayers and sacrifices of the living

Table 5: Comparison of Religious concepts

Probably the best Biblical example for chronological teaching is found in the story of the two Emmaus disciples. After his resurrection, Jesus joins two disciples who are on their way to Emmaus and walks with them. However, they do not recognize him (Lk 24:16). Jesus asks them about their conversation. Their response is very interesting and shows their misunderstandings and incomplete concepts in regards of the Messiah:

> 'What things?' he asked. 'About Jesus of Nazareth,' they replied. 'He was a prophet, powerful in word and deed before God and all the people. The chief priests and our rulers handed him over to be sentenced to death, and they crucified him; but we had hoped that he was the one who was going to redeem Israel. And what is more, it is the third day since all this took place.' (Lk 24:19-21)

We can summarize their response as follows:
- Jesus was a great prophet: "....powerful in word and deed before God and all the people".
- Jesus should not have died; he should rather have delivered Israel: "....but we had hoped that he was the one who was going to redeem Israel."
- There are doubts about the true identity of Jesus: Is he really the Messiah? Is he the Son of God? Was he merely a prophet?

These same three questions also preoccupy many Muslims. In regards of the Messiah, we can therefore compare their situation with the Emmaus disciples. The following table summarizes this comparison:

The disciples of Emmaus	Muslims
Jesus was a great prophet	Jesus was a great prophet
Was Jesus really the Son of God?	Jesus is not the Son of God
Jesus should not have died	Jesus did not die

Table 6: The disciples of Emmaus

What did Jesus do to correct their incomplete understanding and to lead them into the full knowledge of the truth? – Jesus built on their defective knowledge of the Old Testament to show them step by step why the Messiah had to die: in order to fulfill God's plan of salvation:

> He said to them, 'How foolish you are, and how slow of heart to believe all that the prophets have spoken! Did not the Christ have to suffer these things and then enter his glory? And beginning with Moses and all the Prophets, he explained to them what was said in all the Scriptures concerning himself. (Lk 24:25-27) In other terms:

- Jesus taught the Word of God chronologically, starting with the Pentateuch and the Old Testament prophets.

7. Communicating without Words

- Jesus did not teach the whole Old Testament; he rather taught those events and prophecies that either foreshadowed or announced his coming. He did a selective study to highlight to them the foundational concepts of the Old Testament and to show them that its sacrificial system one day would demand a perfect human sacrifice.
- He proved through the Old Testament that he was the Messiah and that he had to die as the Messiah.

The result of this method was that their eyes were opened and their hearts burned within them (Lk 24:31-32).

It was only on the Old Testament background that the disciples were able to really grasp who Jesus was and why he had to die. Jesus took all the time to explain them chronologically, so that the disciples could easily follow. As Muslims are in a comparable situation with the two disciples, using a similar method could possibly lead to similar results.

In Scripture, the foundational concepts are taught over and over again, starting at the first pages. The following table shows some of these most important concepts. The four stories in the four columns are just examples to show how these basic concepts are evidenced:

Basic Biblical Concept seen in...	Creation narrative	Noah	Sacrifice of Isaac	Exodus
God acts in the world	Gen 1:1-31; 3:1	Gen 6:17		Ex 3:8
God is great	Gen 1	Gen 8:1		1Ex 14:13
God is faithful to his Word	Gen 1:24	Gen 6:13;7:10		Ex 14:16, 21
God loves man / speaks	Gen 2:18	Gen 6:18	Gen 22:16-18	Ex 20
God is holy and hates sin	Gen 2:16-17	Gen 6:12		Ex 32:7-9
God punishes sin by death	Gen 2:16-17	Gen 6:13		Ex 32:35
God provides a sacrifice	Gen 3:21	Gen 6:21, 8:21	Gen 22:8, 13	Num 21:8
Man is responsible before God	Gen 3:11	Gen 6:11		Num 21:7
Man is lost, sep. from God	Gen 3:23	Gen 7:21		Dt 25:16
Man can only approach God through faith	Gen 4	Gen 6:22,8:20		Num 21:9b

Table 7: Basic biblical concepts

By gradually teaching these concepts through the OT, the following aims will be achieved:
- Through the repetitive teaching of these basic concepts, a foundation of truth is built.
- Muslims will recognize the vital importance of atoning sacrifices. They will understand that forgiveness of sins is not possible without a blood sacrifice.
- Their heart will be prepared for the coming of Jesus as the Messiah. Whereas Muslims believe that "Jesus did not die", the OT speaks repeatedly about the sacrifices of animals as a substitute for man. By sharing this in our stories the concept that "sin leads to death" will root itself deeply in their hearts, and will prepare them in this way to accept the concept of "the Lamb of God who takes away the sin of the world" (Jn 1:29).

The Qur'an does not offer any solution to the problem of sin and guilt. The message of forgiveness, the solution to the problem of sin, therefore is like providing a glass of fresh water in the middle of a desert. It is offering something better than anything which they have ever known before.

The more the glory of the Scriptures and of Jesus radiate, the more controversy tends to disappear. You will find an in-depths presentation of chronological studies in the following books: *Chronological Bible Storytelling – The gentle way to the heart*, by Christel Eric, LCA, 2000. *Sharing the Gospel through Storytelling*, by LaNette Thompson, LCA, 2009

We believe that lots of prayer for our Muslim friends, and offering them good, clean, fresh water is a much better strategy to bless them than confrontational debates. There are a number of additional advantages of chronologically teaching Bible stories:
- Teaching chronologically is not aggressive
- It is easier to remember a story than an intellectual presentation. This is particularly true in societies with an oral tradition;
- God Himself has chosen to reveal his message in a chronological way and through stories. When we read a book or watch a film, we do not begin in the middle. Why would we do this in sharing the message of the Bible?
- By studying the Bible over a longer period of time, in-depths relationships will be created;
- *The natural frame of a family or group of trusted friends which over a longer period of time study God's Word together, is the ideal basis*

for a subsequent house fellowship. Precious group dynamics are developed that could be important for a later stage.

- Everyone is able to tell stories – and everyone loves to hear stories; therefore, even new and relatively inexperienced believers can start to share Good News with their social environment: simply by telling Biblical narratives; for example: "Oh, you are called Adam. Would you like to know what the Holy Scriptures say about your namesake?"

Telling chronological stories is also very appropriate for work among children or illiterate people. It can further be used in the discipleship and training of leaders. They can come to a meeting once a week, the story is told during the meeting and then when they return home, they can share the story with their acquaintances in the village. There is also an oral version of the chronological method (with pictures instead of texts).

How can you start?

- *Build lots of relationships*: Get known among the people. Intentionally deepen relationships with people who accept and respect you. Invite them to your home and spend time with their families.

- *Suggest reading Biblical stories together with them.* In Appendix ……., you find a suggestion of 44 useful stories in Muslim context.

- *Look for an appropriate place*: for example, invite a couple of trusted friends regularly to your house, or go to their house. We already discussed the importance of having an unthreatening and pleasant setting. It is also important to create something regular, for example weekly.

- *Always show great respect for the Holy Scripture:* Do not put the Bible on the floor or amid other books. Use a Bible in which you have not made any notes and in which no verses have been colored.

- *Learn the story yourself:* let your heart be touched afresh by the story. For those co-workers who serve in a foreign language: if you are not yet fluent in that language, write down a summary of the story and learn it by heart.

- *Prepare simple, clear questions* which you will ask the participants during the gathering. It is much more effective if they learn to get answers directly from the Word of God rather than from a human teacher.

- *Prepare and accompany the whole process with a lot of prayer.* If the context permits it, you might pray for the "Baraka" of God on each individual of the group.

Tell stories

Jesus often told stories or taught in parables. We, too, should learn to tell stories. Not everyone will accept a presentation in the form of a sermon; but everyone loves stories, examples and illustrations drawn from the Word of God as well as everyday life. In many ways, this section is similar to the previous. However, while we emphasized the structured, chronological sharing in the previous section, we want to underline in this section all other kinds of stories.

- *Traditional stories from their cultures*

Co-workers who work with people of other cultures should do their own research to discover their proverbs, illustrations, parables and stories. The better he knows this cultural inheritance, the more he can use them as tools of his sharing and really touch their hearts.

- *Illustrations from everyday life*

The importance of cleanliness can be brought out by asking the simple question about washing dishes after a meal. "Do you only clean the outside? Is it not much more important to have the inside of cups and plates cleaned?" – Likewise, simply washing ones hands, feet, nose is surely good, but how can we obtain a pure heart!?

- *Illustrations from the Word of God*

You can identify the subjects which fascinate them and lead them a step further in their discovery of the Messiah. Here are some examples of subjects which interest Muslims:

  o The life of a prophet: the story of the sacrifice of the son of Abraham (Abraham is well known and loved in the Qur'an). If we say, "Jesus the Son of God died on a cross for our sins," we will be sure to start a big debate. If we tell the story of the son of Abraham, however, everyone will approve the fact that the ram died in place of the son (don't enter the debate whether this son was Isaac or Ishmael, this is not important for now). We can add, "The son of Abraham could not save himself; God had to bring a solution. His solution was a substitute which died in the place of Abraham's son. In the same way, we cannot save ourselves. Therefore God sent a substitute to save us from death. He is Jesus the Messiah." Presenting the Gospel in such a way will allow them to "swallow" something which is usually difficult for them to admit.

  o Forgiveness of sins. Many Muslims ask forgiveness for their sins every day, but they have no assurance that they have ob-

7. Communicating without Words

tained it. Tell stories of people who were forgiven, e.g. the woman caught in adultery (Jn 8:1-11).

- Healings and deliverances: e.g. the paralyzed man brought to Jesus by his friends (Lk 5:17-26) who was then forgiven and healed.
- Stories and parables in regards of the last day of the great judgment: e.g. the rich man and Lazarus in Luke 16:19-31 or the rich fool in Luke 12:13-21.

- *Simple stories that summarize the Biblical drama*

You find an example for such a simply way of presenting the Gospel in the Appendix.

- *Share your own story*

It is rather easy to dispute over doctrine or theology - it is more difficult to argue a concrete personal experience. Sharing a personal, authentic testimony is an effective way of bringing Good News to other people. We should always be prepared to do that, following this passage:

> Always be prepared to give an answer to everyone who asks you to give the reason for the hope that you have. But do this with gentleness and respect. (1Pet 3:15)

Be aware that a Muslim usually defines his relationship with God as one of a slave to his master. A slave is supposed to do what his master tells him, without actually having a personal relationship with him. When you share personal experiences with a personal God, you really have a message to tell!

Therefore, share naturally your own experiences in conversations. Share what you have experienced and what you are experiencing every day with your Lord, such as for example how you experience forgiveness for your sins, peace in your heart, assurance of eternal life, freedom from occult bondages and bad habits, how God leads you and provides for you, how he gives you the strength to forgive other people and to overcome temptation. May be you have experienced how God healed you or one of your friends through prayer. Share these wonderful things with them and invite them to make the same kind of experiences in their own life. The story about how you actually began your journey with Jesus can of course be particularly important. Take note of the following three main points when you share this:

- Emphasize the reasons that made you accept the Good News and become a follower of Jesus.
- Explain precisely how you started to follow Jesus. This will be very new to a Muslim.

- Tell him what has changed in your life since then. Emphasize that life with God is not a blind obedience to the will of God, but rather a relationship of friendship and love. Also, you can witness to him that you regularly have new experiences with your Lord (hopefully every day!).

Sharing your story will give him appetite to experience the same. Encourage him to simply ask God in Jesus name to give him the same experience of peace, forgiveness and joy.

Look out for "landing-strips"

We have already discussed the general felt needs and unanswered questions of many Muslims. We should now get to know the individual who is facing us, so that we can know *his or her specific needs* and how the gospel can have an impact on him/her at this precise moment. Unmet needs are like "runways", entry points for God's blessing in that particular life. The message of the Gospel itself always remains the same; its content cannot be altered. However, *the approach, the formulation, the points which we emphasize can and should be adapted according to each situation.* Jesus spoke with different people in different ways, he used various entry points:

- John 1: Nathanael: use of a word of knowledge that brought him to saving faith (47-49).
- John 3: Nicodemus: a theological debate with answers and questions that brought him to saving faith
- John 4: the Samaritan woman: how and where to worship God. The Samaritan woman is by the way a beautiful example of progressive revelation. In the beginning, she only understood very fragmentary who Jesus really was – however, Jesus adapted his message to her and led her step by step to a full revelation: v. 12 (an ordinary man), v. 19 (a prophet), v. 29 (is he the Messiah?), v. 42 (the Savior of the world).

Paul followed the same model:

- Acts 17: 2-3: in a Jewish context: shares on the basis of Scriptures
- Acts 14: 15-17: in a Gentile context: supernatural healings as entry point
- Acts 17: 22-23: in the philosophic Athens: a reference to a known philosopher as entry point.

The exact entry point or "runway" will vary from individual to individual. Trust in God to prepare such landing strips. Here is an example how a Western gospel messenger created such a "landing":

Every morning I went to the local shop to get some bread for our breakfast. On the way I saw a young man who said to me: "Good morning white man, couldn't you help me to get a visa for America?" I answered him: "Good morning my friend, unfortunately I am not American, so I cannot help you with a visa for America, but I could help you to get a visa to enter paradise. This visa will be granted to everybody who applies for it with his whole heart, and the best thing is: it is free of charge." The man came closer to me and said: "Could I come and visit you this afternoon in private?" "Of course", was my answer and I showed him my house. In the afternoon the man came to my house and told me that he had been praying to God for many years that he would send somebody who would talk to him about Jesus. The man accepted Jesus' big invitation and within a few weeks led one of his close friends to Jesus. I was very touched to see how God had prepared these two people for the Gospel message. Since then I have been praying many times that God would give me wisdom through his Holy Spirit to create natural bridges in everyday situations.

Use the Scriptures

- *Use the Bible*

Do you know the Bible? Your authority is not to be found in your own nice words, but in the Word of God. You should know where important passages and stories are found so that you can recite an appropriate verse or tell an appropriate story at an appropriate moment. Muslims are generally impressed by the simple and clear story of creation, the Ten Commandments, Proverbs and the Psalms, the Sermon on the Mount (where Jesus teaches on three of the five pillars of Islam) or stories of miracles performed by Jesus.

- *Use the Qur'an*

Do you know the Qur'an? As we said in a previous section, truths from the Qur'an can be used as a bridge to Muslims. However, we do not aim at studying the Qur'an, but at reaching the Muslims' heart by using the bridge he loves so dearly. All truth is God's truth, wherever it is to be found. You should therefore know the biblical truth reflected in the Qur'an.

In other situations, you will notice that Muslims may fervently assert a position which is contrary to the Bible and the Qur'an. In this case, their own book may correct them. One typical example for this is the widespread argument among Muslims that the Bible has seemingly been corrupted. This is an affirmation without any foundation. Quite the opposite, the Qur'an views the books which came before (the Taurat, the Zabur and the Injil) very highly. Several times in the Qur'an, we read that it is impossible that the revealed scriptures could be changed (Sura 10:64 and 6:34); that they are revealed by God; that all Muslims are supposed to believe in them.

When you use the Qur'an, don't forget to always use an Arabic version. If you do not speak any Arabic, then purchase a combined edition English-Arabic. Only the Arabic text of the Qur'an has binding authority for a Muslim. Let the Muslim read in the Arabic version himself and follow in the English explanation.

When using the Qur'an, show respect to it. Do not leave it, for example, on the floor or under other books. Muslims always show respect for the Qur'an. It is often covered with a cloth or with leather, and they always put it on the highest place in a room.

Learn to explain the way of salvation

Sooner or later the moment will come for you to help your listener to accept Jesus' big invitation. You should be prepared to present the message of salvation in a simple and clear way. An effective way to do it is the illustration of the bridge, because it summarizes briefly and clearly the basic points of the Gospel:

– Man and God live in perfect unity and have an excellent relationship

– The Fall; the relationship between God and man is broken; the wall between God and man cannot be overcome by any human efforts

– Through religious activities (e.g. the five pillars, good works), Adam and all men after him try to restore the broken relationship – but without any success.

– God himself brings the solution – the perfect man Jesus Christ brings the perfect sacrifice for the guilt of all humans. This sacrifice overcomes the wall of separation.

– Man must accept God's offer and can, through becoming a follower of Jesus, restore his relationship with God.

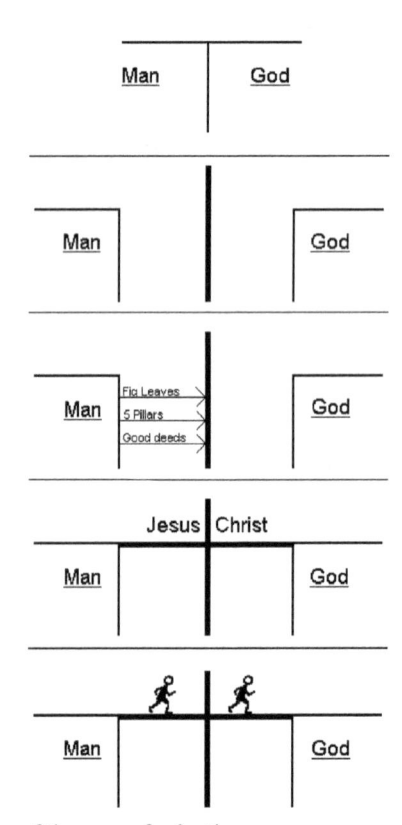

Figure 7: Diagram of the way of salvation

7. Communicating without Words

There are of course many other ways, through which Jesus' big invitation can be explained to a receptive person, including the parables of the two lost sons in Luke 15 or of the broad and the narrow ways in Matthew 7.

Use appropriate media

Media can be an additional "runway", a good entry point for the sharing of Good News. They are also another non-aggressive means, because Muslims can read or watch them quietly, without taking too many risks. Media are quiet messengers at our side.

Some media may be good per se, but not appropriate for our context. We should therefore carefully evaluate them before using them. These two fundamental questions should be asked:

- Does this sort of media suit the people we seek to reach; is it appropriate in their context?
- Is the content of this media biblical?

Before using a media, you should get to know it. For example, before giving a book to someone, it would be good to read it yourself. Before watching a movie with others, watch it yourself. Then, try to find out where the individual stands. Some Islamic sects for example reject everything which is connected to pictures or the representation of people and prophets. It would be better to only give them something written in Arabic and without illustrations. On the other hand, in many oral cultures, movies and simple, illustrated booklets are very popular and therefore effective. The following media can be helpful:

- *Literature*: books, booklets, Gospels, tracts, correspondence courses. Use literature which was written for their context, such as for example biographies of Muslims who have decided to accept Jesus' invitation;
- *Radio and TV:* we can communicate to our friends the times and frequencies of helpful programs;
- *Audio cassettes and Mega-Voices:* Particularly co-workers in rural, poorer areas will soon notice that people love to listen to cassettes and Mega-Voices (a technical device for listening to a message) in their language. Biblical messages or just stories, testimonies and contextual music are all very precious elements.
- *Video cassettes and DVDs:* This media is also very popular in rural areas. Sometimes whole villages gather to watch a movie on the life of Jesus or "God's Story", particularly if it is shown in their mother tongue. This means can effectively be used for family oriented shar-

ing of the Good News. A particularly effective DVD is "More than Dreams" in which several Muslims tell their personal story on how they met Jesus.

- *The Internet:* Communicate to your friends websites or chat rooms through which they can learn more about the Gospel and interact with Christians.

Spread the news as widely as possible

The farmer who kneels down besides his field and earnestly prays to God for an abundant harvest will most likely not reap anything if he does not also sow the seed. The same principle applies to the Word of God: Only if it is sown widely will certain seeds fall on fertile ground and produce fruit; *where there is a lot of sowing, there will also be a lot of reaping.*

It is not possible to sow widely and openly in every context. In some contexts, it can be done without serious consequences, but one should carefully consider whether it is wise to do it, as it may affect the ministry of other workers negatively. In still other contexts it perfectly acceptable (eg. through radio or literature distribution) and it should be done to get the word out.

In certain countries for instance, the Arabic version of the Jesus Film can be shown publicly and with the official authorization of the local government. In other contexts, ten thousands of New Testaments were distributed. In still other contexts, radio programs or the distribution of free videos were effectively used, or the public reading and sharing of God's Word. You need a good combination of wisdom, prudence, boldness and courage to use the opportunities before you.

You particularly need divine wisdom, as too public methods can sometimes have counterproductive effects such as provoking unnecessary persecution. For most contexts, we recommend a "half-public" setting. We define "half-public" the setting of trusted friends and family. If the Good News is shared sensitively and non-aggressively it should be okay in most contexts to do this in a family setting. There are no secrets in this context, and if an extended family decides to accept Jesus' invitation together, the risk of persecution will be diminished considerably.

Open air or public presentations of Good News should only be done if the local authorities (village chief, district governor) give the official permission. Ideally, it is done on invitation by a local sponsor. Preaching or movie nights can be accompanied by prayer for the sick and the oppressed. As a next step, interested people can be invited to discuss the subject further in discreet small groups, possibly in the sponsor's house or in the house of other men of peace.

Celebrate feasts with your Muslim friends

Religious feasts are sometimes other good "runways" to share Good News with Muslims.

- *Muslim feasts*

There are several important feasts in the Muslim calendar. The biggest Islamic feast is the *Eid-ul-Adha / Eid-al-Kabir*, during which Muslims remember Abraham's sacrifice of his son. Each family slaughters a sheep. The meat is shared with neighbors and friends, and Muslims visit, greet and bless each other. It is good for you to participate in these festivities. You might even have the opportunity to explain the deeper meaning of the feast: it was not necessary for Abraham's son to die because God himself provided a solution, a sacrifice to replace him.

Another occasion is the ninth month of the Islamic calendar, the month of Ramadan, when Muslims fast. During this month, many Muslims seek after additional revelations of God, particularly during the 27th night. According to the Islamic Tradition, the Hadiths, it is during this night that Muhammad received the Qur'an. You might possibly have the opportunity, at a visit during this evening, to share with them more divine revelation, for example dreams and visions from the *Injil*.

Fasting itself can be a good "runway", as it is an obligation for every Muslim to fast a whole month per year. Would this possibly be an opportunity for you to explain to a Muslim the Good News that our salvation is not dependant on our works, but rather on God's grace in Jesus the Messiah?

- *Christian feasts*

In the Christian calendar, particularly Christmas and Easter are great opportunities for an in-depth contact with people of other cultures. As a co-worker among Muslims, you can for instance organize a contextual Christmas celebration in your home and invite a few of your acquaintances. During a relaxed meal or tea you may explain the deeper meaning of Christmas. Another possibility is to invite them into your home to watch a good movie which explains Christmas, for example the Jesus Film (this film is particularly appropriate because it has been translated in many languages) or "More than Dreams". After the evening, you might give them a card with a meaningful verse or a good book that they can read at home. The same principles can be applied at Easter.

Most Muslims might not be able to attend a traditional church to be present at your celebrations. However, they might willingly accept an invitation to come to your home and spend some extended time with you. If they do not come, you could still send them a meal or a few sweets to share your joy with them.

Work through proximate believers

In many contexts today it is possible to work through "proximate believers" in order to bless ever more Muslims. Proximate believers are followers of Christ who live closely to Muslims.

- *Proximate believers from a Muslim background*

Believers from a Muslim background are of course ideally positioned to bless people from their own or a similar cultural and social background with the Good News. You might perhaps know the Bible better than him, but he is the one who knows better than anyone in the world the customs, the social structure and the way his people do things. Therefore, if you hear about believers of the same background as the people you try to reach, get council from them. Work together with them. Let them introduce you in the culture and customs of their own people. However, you might also help them to progress: share with them, build them up, give them further teaching, show them how they can be a real blessing to their people – work with them and through them.

- *Proximate believers from a Christian or Animistic background*

Many contexts in Asia and Africa have significantly changed over the last few decades: in quite a few areas, the church of Christ has strongly multiplied, so that today, literally Millions of true followers of Jesus Christ live in Sub-Saharan Africa and Asia. In Africa, there are approx. 430 Mio Muslims and 180 Mio Evangelicals, whereas in Asia, there are approx. 150 Mio Evangelicals and 1,1 Bio Muslim. In many regions, Evangelical Christians live in more or less immediate proximity to Muslim people groups which have never heard about the Good News in Jesus Christ. In these contexts, it can be most effective to also coach, train and facilitate co-workers from a Christian or Animistic background in addition to your personal work with Muslims. By doing this, you tap into the potential of significantly multiplying your efforts. We recommend the book *"Releasing the workers of the 11th hour – the Global South and the task remaining"*, William Carey, Pasadena, CA, by the same author. This book shows various practical ways through which you can work in partnership with proximate believers.

Bless people through compassion ministries

Again, we want to emphasize how important it is to bless people by acts of love. If you have the means to do so, start projects to bless Muslims in your area. There are of course countless ways to do this. Some ideas for those in a Western context who work with immigrants: offering language lessons of the national language, helping newcomers through cultural orientation courses, encouraging academically weak students through extra-lessons etc.

Co-workers in Africa or Asia could for instance think of small or large scale projects in the areas of education (literacy, learning centers, IT and English courses), rural development (agricultural, reforestation), health (vaccination programs, primary health care, mobile clinics) or economic self-reliance programs (micro-credit, micro-business).

Learn to answer sensitive questions

A co-worker who is involved with people of other cultures and Religions will regularly be confronted with sensitive questions. It is important that he learns to answer these questions in a competent and biblical way. This area of study is called "Apologetics", from Greek "*Apologia*", defense.

In our experience, most arguments brought forth by Muslims can be summarized in approx. ten areas. The co-worker who knows these ten areas of conflict or questions and how to respond to them, will normally not have any additional problems when communication with Muslims. There are dozens of books on the topic of "Apologetics" – we recommend to you to study some of them in order to have competent answers.

Most Muslims have particular difficulties with the Biblical Christology. How is it possible for a human being to be Son of God? How can God be three in one? It might be helpful to explain that no true follower of Jesus has ever affirmed that Jesus was the physical Son of God. Jesus is not the physical, but rather the spiritual Son of God (through a miracle, Jesus came directly through the Holy Spirit in Mary's womb). It was not the Christians who said that Jesus was the Son of God, but rather God himself affirmed this on several occasions. Whoever really submits himself to God should accept what God Himself declared about Jesus. The term "Son of" does not necessarily imply physical descendant. Arabs know the term "Ibn is sabil", which literally means "son of the road". This term does not mean that the road had sexual relations that produced a son; rather it simply has a metaphorical meaning. Likewise, "son of God" has a metaphorical or spiritual, not a physical meaning.

Many Muslims assume that Christians believe in three gods, because they talk about the Trinity. It might be helpful to explain that no true follower of Jesus believes in three gods. Muslims believe in the "99 beautiful names of Allah". Does this mean that Muslims believe in 99 gods? No, it rather means that Allah has revealed himself in 99 wonderful ways. Similarly, Christians believe that God has revealed himself in three glorious ways as Father, Son and Holy Spirit. To use a human example: Ali sells fruit in his grocery. At home, he is the father of two children. As a hobby, he is the president of a volunteer's club. Are there three Ali's? – No, but the same and unique Ali has three different roles as a vendor, father and president.

These were just two examples as a way to illustrate apologetics. We would again like to encourage you to do more research on this topic so that you will have really good answers to the sincere questions of Muslims. We recommend the book *Christian-Islamic Controversy* by Gerhard Nehls and Walter Eric, LCA, Kenya.

8
The Big Invitation

In this chapter, we will discuss the third phase of our diagram: the invitation. We are not in a position to force anyone to accept this invitation. However, it is nonetheless our task and calling to make this invitation to all people as attractive as ever possible.

To return to our illustration of construction: this third step would correspond to the roof. If we stopped building after finishing the foundation and the walls, our efforts would have been futile. But if we put on a pretty roof without a good foundation and without walls, that would also be pointless. In our work with people of other cultures and religions, we should not seek quick decisions, but in due time the day must come when we clearly announce the Good News, inviting the person to make the right decision.

There is, of course, a tension in this: On the one hand, no-one can ever accept Jesus' big invitation without the Almighty God himself drawing him to Jesus (Jn 6:44); On the other hand, we are called to follow Paul's example who reasoned and debated with the Jews and the Gentiles with the aim of convincing them to accept this invitation (Acts 9:29; 17:2, 17; 18:4, 19; 19:8-9).

We should therefore fully assume our responsibility and do our best to present the Good News in an acceptable and culturally-sensitive way (like a trader presents his merchandise in a way to give potential customers the desire to buy it. We will find it easier to buy from a trader who is kind and tidy and presents his goods in an ordered and clean way). We can and must present the truth and overcome every cultural and social obstacle which could get in the way, but we cannot and should not force anyone to accept the big invitation.

So, in reality, it is not us, but Jesus himself who invites. Several verses speak about Jesus' big invitation:

> If anyone is thirsty, *let him come* to me and drink. (Jn 7:37b)
>
> *Come to me,* all you who are weary and burdened. (Mat 11:28)
>
> Let the little children *come to me*, and do not hinder them. (Mat 19:14)
>
> *Come*, for everything is now ready. (Lk 14:17)
>
> The Spirit and the bride say: *Come!* And let him who hears say, *Come!* Whoever is thirsty, *let him come*. (Rev 22:17)

We are like the servants in Jesus' parable of the King's wedding banquet (Mat 22:1-14). These servants were sent out by the King "to those who had been invited to the banquet to tell them to come" (V. 3). He asks us to go to all possible and impossible places and to invite all that we will find (V. 9); and Rev 22:17 highlights that whoever hears Jesus' big invitation is automatically called to extend this invitation to others: "And let him who hears say, Come!"

Accepting the invitation is often a process

The messenger pursues this goal: the listener should not only hear about the invitation, but also accept it.

Accepting the big invitation has three basic elements: faith in Jesus Christ (Acts 16:31), repentance (Acts 3:19 – repentance means "to turn away from" and "to turn towards") and verbal confession (Rom 10:9-10).

Accepting the big invitation has three immediate consequences: a new spiritual birth (Jn 3), forgiveness of sins (Acts 3:19), and assurance of eternal life (1Jn 5:11-13).

On paper, all this looks quite simple and straightforward. In real life, however, accepting the big invitation has various aspects, and often we may not be sure who is "in" and who is "out".

To start with, let us be clear that a simple verbal confession is not to be confused with an authentic acceptance of Jesus' invitation. It is important to note that every Muslim "believes" in Jesus. Actually, every Muslim has to believe in Jesus to be a real Muslim. Therefore, to believe in Jesus and to really follow Jesus are two rather different pairs of shoes.

We should also be aware of the fact that for many Muslims accepting Jesus' invitation is not a unique event in their lives, but rather a slow process. During this process the three elements mentioned above will surely take place. However, when and where exactly they do, the person herself may not be able to say. Often, the culminating point of this process is water baptism.

Jesus has addressed this issue in some of his Kingdom parables. For example, in Matthew 13:29-30, he states that the wheat and the weeds grow together until the end, and only at the end will there be a big separation. In Matthew 13:33 we read about the yeast that will work through the whole dough. And in Matthew 13:47-49, Jesus says that the good and the bad fish are all together in the same net, and it will only be at the end that the angels will separate (note: the angels, not well intending Christians!).

These parables show that it is possibly less our task as human beings to define who is good and who is bad, who is in and who is out. Rather, it is our task to implant the Gospel, like seed, into the hearts of individuals and entire families.

8. The Big Invitation

Like yeast in the dough, it should then expand from within and bless whole families, peoples, entire cultures and draw them closer to God.

During this process, as Jesus is realized more and more as Savior and Lord, his principles will more and more become the foundation of their lives, and their love for him will grow more and more, and eventually influence all their decisions. Accepting the invitation is therefore only a first step in a long process which will last a lifetime, and through which people learn to become more and more what they are called to be.

Different motives

We can distinguish between the following three categories of motives:

- *Selfish or political motive: the hope for a better life*

    A man with leprosy came to him and begged him on his knees, 'If you are willing, you can make me clean.'" (Mk 1:40)

    'What do you want me to do for you?' Jesus asked him. The blind man said, 'Rabbi, I want to see.'" (Mk 10:51)

Jesus did not condemn people with this kind of motive; rather, he accepted them and led them a step further. Most people who come to Jesus are in this first category!

- *God-centered motive: Understanding the greatness and holiness of God*

    'Who are you, Lord,' Saul asked. 'I am Jesus whom you are persecuting,' he replied. (Acts 9:5)

- *Social motive: Search for social well-being and integration (Zachaeus in Luke 19:8-10; Simon in Acts 8:5-25)*

Although Jesus invited people with selfish or social motives to follow him, he clearly showed them the new priorities for their lives: "...seek *first* his Kingdom..." (Mt 6:33)

We can, yes, we are commissioned to share the blessings which Jesus came to bring, e.g. peace, healing, deliverance, assurance of salvation, protection from spirits, forgiveness of sins, direct access to God etc. The desire of man to know these things are a legitimate reason and an acceptable motive for people to come to Jesus.

Therefore, people do not necessarily have to come to Jesus for spiritual reasons – but by the grace of God, they will, during the course of their life, become more spiritual. Jesus spent a considerable amount of time with the worst of sinners of his time and society – in fact they were the best candidates for his message of salvation. This is in no way different today: *People do not have to be good in order to come to Jesus*. This truly is the Good News: People from all backgrounds are invited to come to Jesus, whatever their motives might be, whatever their sins might have been; Jesus says: "Come!" – And once they have come to him, he will not let them stay the way they came. Someone said: *"Christ loves us so much that we can come to him just as we are, but he loves us too much to leave as the way we are."*

Isn't this true for each one of us who have come to Jesus as our Savior and Lord? So, let us not expect more from people of other cultures and religions than from ourselves!

Let us re-emphasize what we already discussed: In societies which are group-orientated, the social motive becomes very important. It will be easier for people from such a background to accept Jesus' invitation in a family or social group, following the Biblical examples of group-oriented people such as the household of Cornelius (Acts 10), the jailer (Acts 16) or Lydia (Acts 16). In these cultures, you should aim at blessing the whole family and accompany them together in this process of drawing slowly closer to the Kingdom of God.

Five important influences during the decision process

Recent research has shown that in many cases, one or several of the following influences have been important for Muslims who decided to accept Jesus' invitation.

Influence	Characteristic	Our adapted contribution
Theological	The greatness and glory of Jesus in the Qur'an and in the Gospel	Show them this glory; encourage them to read and study more to get to know it
Positive	Friendship, practical love and authentic life of a Christian	Be social with them; live out an authentic Christian life for them to observe; show genuine love; be a good witness
Negative	Disillusionment with the fanaticism and extremism of others (e.g. suicide bombers, *sharia* impact = Islamic legislation)	Show to them evidence of this in today's world events; compare and explain the Islamic and Biblical ideals
Supernatural	Dreams and visions; Divine healings	Expect God to stir up Muslims through dreams and visions; and when they occur, interpret them in light of the Word of God; be ready to pray for and with sick people

Influence	Characteristic	Our adapted contribution
Social	Followers of Jesus from same family network or community	Encourage and train believers to share the Good News with their families and social networks

Table 8: Five important influences during the conversion process

The knowledge of these influences can help us to be better prepared when God wants to use us. In most cases, a combination of influences rather than one single factor has helped Muslims to understand and accept the big invitation. No doubt, only rarely do dreams and visions lead a person to accept Jesus' invitation instantly. However, they often are an important influence to get the whole process going.

Various phases of the decision process

It is often a long process that finally leads Muslims to accept Jesus' invitation. A main cause for this is that there are many reasons which hinder them to follow Jesus:

- They do not see any other option to their current situation
- They may not know any other person from their family or social environment who follows Jesus
- They have strong prejudices about Christians and Christianity
- They are under enormous pressure from their community, the *ummah*, which discourages any major change in their lives
- They have never known an authentic follower of Jesus who could have shared Good News with them in a credible way

Let us take a closer look at the various phases of the process:

-8	Knowledge of God, but no effective knowledge of the gospel
-7	Establishes a positive contact with a messenger of the gospel
-6	Corrects prejudices and re-evaluates the concepts and verses of the Qur'an about Jesus
-5	Initial awareness of the Gospel through the life of a messenger
-4	Awareness of the basics of the Gospel through the Scriptures
-3	Understanding of the implications of the Gospel for him
-2	Recognition of a personal need for salvation and for a Savior
-1	Invitation and decision to follow Christ
0	Acceptance of the invitation
+1	Evaluation of the decision
+2	Beginning of a new fellowship of believers or integration into an existing fellowship of believers
+3	Active participation

Table 9: The phases of the process

It is your task to take the Muslim by the hand and lead him one step closer to a real understanding of Jesus the Messiah. Wherever you meet Muslims, put something into their lives. Perhaps someone else will lead them again a step further. Equally, you might sometimes meet Muslims that have already gone many steps and are now ready to accept Jesus' big invitation.

The Bible reports how individuals (Acts 8:30), whole families (Acts 10:24.47; 16:30-33) or even whole villages (Acts 9:35) accepted Jesus' invitation.

The phase + 1 can be crucial. It will possibly only be after some time that a new follower of Jesus will be aware of the real implications of his decision. He might have experienced some first difficulties, disappointments, or even persecutions. He will therefore re-evaluate his decision and possibly have to decide a second time with full knowledge of the facts to accept once and for all the consequences of his decision. It is at this time that they particularly need to be encouraged and surrounded by other, more mature believers.

We have already discussed the importance of accompanying entire families. Muslims view themselves as a part of a social group, the *ummah*, and we should not seek to alienate them from this community. The more such big decisions are made as a group, the more they have a strong chance of lasting. Groups will of course need more time to reach a consensus. However, it is worthwhile to give them that time. Therefore, be on good terms with those in society who have the capacity to make important decisions and show them all necessary respect. If they view you as a trustworthy, godly person, they might be able to accept or even approve, when people from their group decide to follow the Messiah.

Confessions of authentic faith

Authentic faith expresses itself through the following three confessions:

Verbal Confession ("Jesus is my Lord" – Rom 10:9-10)

Confessions of Authentic Faith

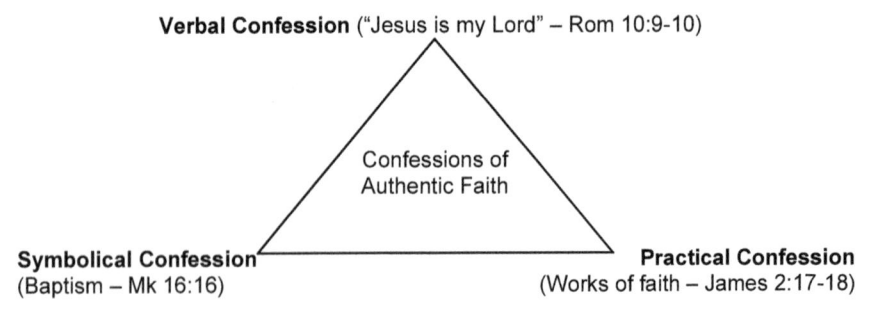

Symbolical Confession
(Baptism – Mk 16:16)

Practical Confession
(Works of faith – James 2:17-18)

Figure 8: Confessions of authentic faith

The reality of these three confessions in the life of a person is evidence that there is authentic faith in his heart, that he is an authentic follower of Jesus. A daily, ongoing reality of these three confessions is more important than a onetime event.

9
Growing as a Follower of Jesus

Whoever has accepted Jesus' big invitation will be eager to learn and to grow as his follower. This leads us to the fourth phase of our diagram: participation. To come back to our illustration of a house construction: this phase would correspond to the training of our "assistant builders", so that they too can "build houses". If we are the only builders, we will not get very far, because our capacity is too limited. But if we train *others* to also build houses, multiplication can take place. Growing as a follower of Jesus can also be compared with the physical and emotional growth of children. When they are born, they are completely dependent on outside help. They need lots of love, care and tenderness. They also need food and clothing. If we neglect them, they will die! As they grow, they learn how to walk. In the process of learning to walk, babies repeatedly lose their balance and fall. But each time they fall they get up and try again. It is by falling that they learn to walk. No parent would hit them, when they fall. On the contrary, they will rejoice and encourage them towards each new step. This is how we should accompany new followers of Jesus. Without doubt, they will at times fall back into old sinful behavior patterns. How could we expect them to automatically apply Biblical behavior patterns! They might disappoint and fail us. However, that does not mean that they have deceived or betrayed us. Instead of assuming the worst, it would be better to do everything to pick them up and continue to accompany them patiently.

Focus on the most urgent problems

The new believer will have to deal with theological, social, spiritual, legal, and identity issues.

- *Theological conflicts*
    - Who really is Jesus? Is he just a great prophet, possibly greater than others, or is he actually the Son of God? – Many Muslims will at first recognize Jesus as Messiah and Savior, and possibly only in subsequent phases also accept his divine nature. I know a believer from a Muslim background who said that he was a genuine follower of Jesus, but it took him eight years to feel comfortable when saying "Jesus is the Son of God."

- What really is the Qur'an? What authority does it have?
- Who really is Muhammad? – At the end of a course at a Bible school one of the students from a Muslim background asked: "Will Muhammad also be in heaven?"

- *Social challenges*
  - How do I define my relationship with the *ummah* now that I follow Christ?
  - Is it possible to keep my social position within my family and social network? If yes, how?

- *Spiritual ignorance*
  - What are the "five pillars" of my new religious practice? – Before becoming a follower of Jesus, he always knew what was expected of him: wash his hands before prayer or opening the Qur'an, say "*al-hamdulillah*" when someone sneezes, etc. Now he asks: "What does God expect from an authentic follower of Jesus?"
  - How do I protect myself from evil spirits? – Before, he was told to trust in charms or other protective mechanisms. Now he needs to learn how to deal biblically with spiritual bondage and how to live in freedom from fear.

- *Legal consequences*
  - Do I have the legal right to follow Jesus? – In certain countries, young people who are under 18 years of age do not have the right to make religious decisions; in other places, the choice to follow Jesus is considered blasphemous (apostasy laws).

- *The identity issue*
  - Do I have to call myself a Christian in order to follow Jesus? – A study of the Book of Acts shows that "Christians" received various titles (followers of the Way, believers, brothers, saints) and the title "Christian" simply was a nickname given to the "Jesus people" (see Acts 11:26).
  - Do I have to go to an established church (building) in order to be part of God's family? *You may want to stop reading for a moment and reflect or discuss with others some of the practical implications of these issues.*

9. Growing as a Follower of Jesus

Seek biblical answers to crucial questions

When a Muslim accepts Jesus' big invitation, he will have many questions that need to be answered at an early stage: Is it permissible to continue practicing some of the 5 pillars? May I continue reciting the confession of faith (*shahada*)? Should I still keep the fast during Ramadan? Do I have to eat pork as a Christian? – There are many other questions puzzling the mind of a new believer. Let us establish some principles by looking at a few of these issues.

- *The Five Pillars*

Because most of these pillars are practiced daily, it becomes very obvious to the community when a Muslim stops practicing them. Perhaps in urban settings and in areas where people are not really following and practicing the pillars these issues are less of a problem. But in other areas where Muslims follow Islam as a close-knit community these questions are very important and need to be addressed.

As a general rule we advise believers not to say or to practice what they don't believe in their hearts. Each believer should follow Jesus with his whole heart and stay clear from a life-style that will be perceived as deceptive.

- *Reciting the confession of faith (shahada)*

For new believers who have come out of a background of strict religious adherence just dropping all ritual practice might lead to an inner void and uncertainty. This could possibly be filled by using a contextualized confession of faith, as for example 1Timothy 2:5 or Philippians 2:5-11, or other passages that give us creedal confessions of the early church. "For there is one God, and one mediator between God and men, the man Christ Jesus", certainly is such a creedal statement.

Some new believers might want to refer to themselves as "Muslims" with the understanding that this is a cultural and social rather than religious identification. We believe they too should be encouraged to communicate verbally and by their actions that their primary identity is as a follower of Jesus Christ.

- *What about praying, fasting alongside with Muslims?*

These are not easy questions that can be dealt with in general answers or instructions. The Christian worker who seeks to guide new believers from an Islamic background will be very unwise in taking decisions for or strongly influencing the new believer. While they will not want to encourage him to become estranged from his/her cultural and social network, we are all well aware that our loyalty to Jesus is of primary importance. As one such new believer recalled how in the midst of his family's intense accusations of forsaking his roots and not honoring even his mother who had given life to him he clearly heard a voice in between his sobs and tears: "He who honors father or mother more than me is not worthy of me…(Matthew 10:37-39).

We should often look for answers together with the new believers in the Word of God. In Matthew 10:33 we read this radical statement: "But whoever disowns me before men, I will disown him before my Father in heaven." What does this verse mean for a new believer? It is certainly not the task of the discipler to tell the new believer when and how he should take a public stand for Jesus.

For some believers it means that they should break instantly and completely with all forms of Muslim prayer, fasting, ritual cleansing or going to the mosque, as not to do so *in their understanding* would mean to deny Jesus. For others it means to continue performing the ritual prayers, fast during the month of Ramadan, and to go to the mosque. *In their spiritual understanding* they do not feel they deny Jesus this way. They still practice the outward Islamic forms, but yet submit themselves in Spirit and truth to God in the name of Jesus. They continue fasting, but their motivation for doing so has changed. They are no longer fasting to gain merit from performing good deeds, but they thank God that they have received forgiveness of their sins in Jesus. And they may still go to the mosque so that they might not be excluded from their immediate community as this would hinder them to share the Good News in their social network.

Of course, sooner or later they will want to confess their loyalty to God's family and their new identity in Christ, but the Christian worker should not push them to do so before they have found a viable spiritual position in which they can do this with conviction and confidence.

- *Difficulties are normal*

The believer needs to know that difficulties are part of following Jesus. Since Jesus was persecuted, beaten and finally killed, therefore his followers will have to suffer in similar ways as well. It is very important that the new believer doesn't have to suffer because he is considered of having "betrayed his culture" or of having "become part of western society". He should only suffer because of his faith in Jesus and not because of any other reasons.

Conclusion: The believer's first loyalty is Jesus himself. Christians from existing churches should not challenge this primary loyalty by pressurizing them into joining a traditional church; nor should the new believer allow him/herself to compromise his/her loyalty to Jesus. Believers need our guidance and assistance in these crucial issues. Answers and ways need to be found together with the believers considering the principles of the Bible and through the guidance of the Holy Spirit. *We are well advised to remind ourselves that the "heart-*

direction" of the believer is what matters most even though his outward practices may irritate or sow doubts in the minds of traditional believers.

Thus the Christian discipler will first and foremost look for the key-signs of growth and ask:

- o Does the person really love Jesus?
- o Can we see the fruit of the Holy Spirit in his life?
- o Does the person read the Bible?
- o Does the person regularly pray to God in the name of Jesus?
- o Does the person share the new life in words and deeds with others?

> *It is not of primary importance, whether a person worships God „in Samaria or in Jerusalem", it is important that s/he worships God in "spirit and in truth" (cp. John 4).*

Don't forsake your God-given socio-cultural identity

Let us reflect somewhat more on this vital issue. New followers of Jesus should be encouraged not to forsake their socio-cultural identity. Following Christ does not mean to embrace the typical Western form of Christianity. The New Testament brings out clearly that new believers from a non-Jewish culture were not required to leave their original identity in order to follow Jesus. They did not have to fulfill or keep the laws of Judaism (Acts 15 and others). Also, in John 4, Jesus showed the Samaritan woman that God is more concerned about genuine, authentic worship "in spirit and in truth" (John 4:23) than conducting this worship service in a specific place (in Jerusalem or in Samaria) at a fixed time (Sabbath days or "Sundays only"). The Samaritan woman was never requested by Jesus to give up her Samaritan culture or identity, but was reminded to worship God in spirit and in truth. Likewise, the Roman Centurion Cornelius was not required to first get circumcised, so that he could follow Jesus (Acts 10). Consequently Paul taught the Corinthian believers that they should remain in the status and in the identity each of them had prior to their decision to follow Jesus:

> Nevertheless, each one should retain the place in life that the Lord assigned to him and to which God has called him. This is the rule I lay down in all the churches. Was a man already circumcised when he was called? He should not become uncircumcised. Was a man uncircumcised when he was called? He should not be circumcised. Circumcision is nothing and uncircumcision is nothing. Keeping God's commands is what counts. Each one should remain in the situation which he was in when God called him....Brothers, each man, as responsible to God, should remain in the situation God called him to. (1Cor 7:17-20.24; cp. Gal 6:15)

A Jesus-follower is therefore not supposed to leave his socio-religious context; rather, he should work towards "redeeming" it! Many Muslims have a strong socio-religious-cultural identity: to be Arab means to be a Muslim. To be Malay means to be a Muslim. So, to officially become a "Christian" would mean that they are not allowed any longer to be Arab or Malay. However, the good news is: They can, yes, they should remain Arab or Malay, Hausa or Swahili and follow Jesus. *Instead of becoming Western-cultural Christians, their primary calling is to remain in their socio-cultural identity and pursue the transformation of this god-given surroundings from within, like yeast which works all through the dough.*

Please note that the socio-religious birth is determined by God:

> God...determined the times set for them and the exact places where they should live. God did this so that men would seek him and perhaps reach out for him and find him, though he is not far from each one of us. (Acts 17:26-28)

A new believer, in addition to his cultural identity, also has a spiritual identity in Jesus Christ. When the Gospel is implanted into a life, a new spiritual identity is created; this new spiritual identity will transform the socio-cultural identity *without replacing it,* as the following two pictures show:

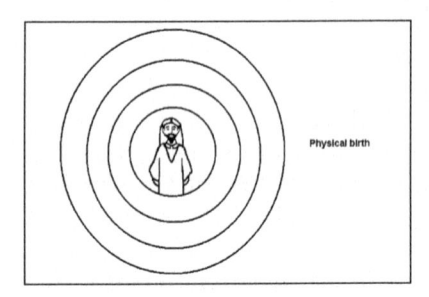

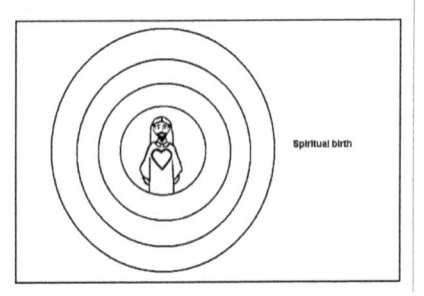

Figure 9: Physical and Spiritual birth

The more we encourage new believers to remain in their god-given environment, the less they will be viewed by it as traitors or as apostates, and the more they can pursue their god-given mandate to bless their family and people. In view of the great divine vision of blessing all families and peoples, it would simply be a too little goal to only invite a few isolated Muslims to follow Jesus. We should rather work towards keeping new followers of Jesus within their context in order to bless it through the Gospel seed and draw it closer to the Savior.

Conclusion: In the New Testament, Greek followers of Jesus did not have to become Jewish in order to follow Jesus. (cp. Acts 15). *In the same way, new believers from a Muslim background do not have to become cultural Chris-*

tians in order to follow Jesus. It is our task to invite them to follow Jesus and then to practice this Biblical faith within their original, God-given context – whenever we do more than this, we have done too much! The goal of discipleship is not to "Christianize", but rather to produce the fruits of the Holy Spirit and spiritual maturity.

Help them to overcome difficulties

Jesus never promised his followers an easy or comfortable life. We should therefore never give the impression that followers of Jesus do not have to face great difficulties. Jesus actually warned his disciples:

> Blessed are you when people insult you, persecute you and falsely say all kinds of evil against you because of me. Rejoice and be glad, because great is your reward in heaven, for in the same way they persecuted the prophets who were before you. (Mt 5:11-12)

Paul also knew about the importance of preparing new believers to face difficulties:

> We must go through many hardships to enter the kingdom of God. (Acts 14:22b)
>
> In fact, everyone who wants to live a godly life in Christ Jesus will be persecuted. (2Tim 3:12)

Therefore, the question is not whether difficulties will arise or not, for we will have to face them in any case. The question is rather how we will overcome these difficulties. Here are a few thoughts:

- *Show them that difficulties are normal and biblical.*
- *Encourage them to persevere.*
- *Show them that nothing in life can ever be more important than following Jesus.*

> Anyone who loves his father or mother more than me is not worthy of me; anyone who loves his son or daughter more than me is not worthy of me; and anyone who does not take his cross and follow me is not worthy of me. Whoever finds his life will lose it, and whoever loses his life for my sake will find it. (Mt 10:37-39)

Each time they are insulted or mistreated, their reward in heaven "increases" (Mt 5:11-12). It will be of particular encouragement to them if they know other believers from the same religious and socio-cultural background that have gone through persecution too and can thus understand their struggles.

- *Surround them and support them in prayer and fasting.* Pray with them and for them and mobilize prayer for them (cp. Col 1:9: "*...we have not stopped...* ").

- *Create an additional social environment for them.*

As we saw in chapter 5, the social environment of a Muslim consists of three layers: the nuclear family, the extended family and the Muslim *ummah*. This environment, this identity he is not supposed to forsake – we should rather work towards creating an additional socio-spiritual context within this God-given environment. This additional context could again consist of three layers:

  o *A trusted friend*: This person is very close to the new believer, like the trusted nuclear family. Often, this trusted friend knows the new believer very well and has possibly already played a part in his process of accepting Jesus' big invitation.

Despite all our precautions and wise strategies, it is sometimes not possible for the new believer to remain in his original environment. If this is the case, the trusted friend becomes to the new believer like a new nuclear family, according to the promise which Jesus made in Mk 10:29-30 and Mt 12:48-50. In this extreme case of harsh persecution nothing can replace this social belonging to a family. Anyone, but especially a new believer, needs not only food and shelter, but also affection, love and *a social belonging*. Most new believers from a Muslim background who backslide do not so for theological, but for social reasons, because they simply miss a meaningful social home. To become the nuclear family to such people does not necessarily mean to live under the same roof, but it means to become as close as a nuclear family.

- *A community of faith*: Whenever possible, this should consist of other believers from his socio-cultural background.

This community of faith should be close to him like the extended family. In this setting, he should be able to relax, have friends, and feel at home culturally and socially. Sunday morning services in a traditional Western setting are not a good place for this. Gatherings and fellowship in a small group of like-minded people from the same socio-cultural context will be of great encouragement for new believers and strengthen their faith.

- *The body of Christ*: The new believer should know that s/he is now part of the large, worldwide family of God. This positive awareness of belonging to a worldwide organism, the body of Christ, should give them security and support that far surpasses the *ummah*.

At a social level, the new follower of Jesus is surrounded by three important social groups represented by these three circles:

9. Growing as a Follower of Jesus 103

Figure 10: The socio-spiritual environment of the new believer

- *Be ready for "Plan B":*

Despite all our cultural sensitivity, our strategic precautions and our fervent prayers, it is sometimes not possible for a new believer to physically remain in his/her nuclear family. As his/her brother/sister in Christ, you should also be prepared for this difficult situation:

- Avoid creating economic dependency. If economic problems are very pressing, treat him/her as a son and not as a beggar.
- If s/he has lost his job because of his faith, support her/him in finding a new job. Pray with your friend and seek together for an appropriate solution that is not dependent on you. Possibly ways of assistance may include to explore training opportunities for new skills that s/he can develop to earn a living.
- If his life itself is in danger, it will perhaps be necessary for him to go elsewhere for a short period of time. However, this place should be as culturally (and geographically) close to his original setting as possible. He must understand that this is only a provisional, short-term solution and that it would be desirable to return to their family as soon as possible. Experience has shown that:
    o Such harsh persecution is in most cases only of a short-term nature, and that a re-integration is possible in many cases. It should therefore be pursued.

- o Life threats are in most cases only verbal. Executions of believers from a Muslim background only happen very rarely (not more often than killings of expatriate gospel witnesses). Nobody can be killed without God's permission and in his time (cp. Lk 4:28–30 with Jn 13:1).

- *Encourage him to overcome evil by good (cp. Rom 12:21).*

- *Encourage them to be particularly loving and loyal to their families and social networks.*

In a first phase, it might be wiser to follow Peter's advice to live in their midst "with gentleness and respect, keeping a clear conscience" (1Pet 3:15-16). The social environment should notice that the character of the new believer has been transformed, that he has become more loving, more patient, more peaceful and humbler than he was before, and this will draw them also to the Savior. Even if in the beginning members of the family are hostile, experience has shown that if new believers behave like respected, exemplary, loving and loyal husbands, brothers, sons, fathers etc., the initial persecution calms down after a certain time. Instead of being expelled by the family, the opposite will happen: like yeast, they will work all through the whole network with the Kingdom of God and slowly draw them to the Messiah.

- *Encourage women to be particularly patient and loyal.*

The situation with women can be particularly delicate, if their husbands or fathers are not sympathetic to the Gospel. In many instances, women and children do not have any religious rights within Islamic cultures. Here a few thoughts:

- o Encourage them to be loyal towards their parents or husbands. According to the Biblical teaching in 1Cor 7:12-16, the believing partner is never supposed to ask for a divorce.

- o Teach them how to live out their Christian life peacefully and respectfully, to obey their husband and live in a pure way (1Pet 3:1-2). They should quietly and peacefully follow Jesus, be more obedient children than ever before, be more loyal wives than ever before and become effectively Good News to their families.

- o Other believers should intentionally seek to establish a positive relationship with the husbands of these wives and implant the Gospel seed into their lives.

Avoid these mistakes

- *Do not expose the new believer by practicing a kind of "hero worship"*. Sometimes, well-intending Christians have publically exposed new believers from a Muslim background by putting them in the limelight. Remember: He is still a spiritual baby and first needs to grow in Christ.

- *Do not provoke difficulties.* There is a persecution which must happen and there is a persecution which we can provoke unwisely and untimely.

- *Do not push him too quickly into a Bible school.* Rather allow him the time to grow and mature within his context and develop a vision, a sense of a personal calling. Bi-vocational training is in most cases preferable to a full-time Bible school.

- *Don't create any economic dependency.* Be careful with economic help. His environment could possibly react very sensitively to this and accuse you of corruption. If you help on an economic level, do it punctually and only be providing an initial set-up capital.

- *Do not promise something which you cannot fulfill later.* Little discouragements at the beginning can cause a relapse and unnecessary frustrations later on.

- *Don't aim at taking him/her out of his/her socio-cultural context.* We have already discussed this principle. Even if there are initial difficulties with his family and *ummah*, the ideal solution for him is not to emigrate to a foreign country (and never come back), but to persevere in faith and loyalty with the one goal of blessing his god-given socio-cultural setting, even if s/he does not seem to like this blessing initially.

- *Don't assume that he has already understood everything.* Even if he uses the correct terminology, it does not mean that he connects the right Biblical content with the words he uses. It might take an extended time for him to really mature spiritually.

- *Never underestimate the spiritual powers.* Especially in Popular Islamic contexts, it is common to work with occult practices. In this type of setting, the new believer should be familiar with Biblical protective mechanisms and learn not to be fearful. He should also learn the basics of apologetics in order to respond competently to difficult questions.

Teach and train new believers

Teaching believers is commanded in the Word of God:

> ...and teaching them to obey everything I have commanded you. (Mt 28:20) And the things you have heard me say in the presence of many witnesses entrust to reliable men who will also be qualified to teach others. (2 Tim 2:2)

Teaching should aim at growth at the following levels:

- *Growth at the level of the vertical relationship:*
    - Knowing how to live his personal relationship with God (listening to the voice of God, praying, obeying etc.)
    - Personal sanctification
- *Growth at the level of the horizontal relationships:*
    - How to be a friendly, faithful member of the society and extended family
    - How to be a friendly, faithful member of a faith community

Teaching new believers has three main dimensions:

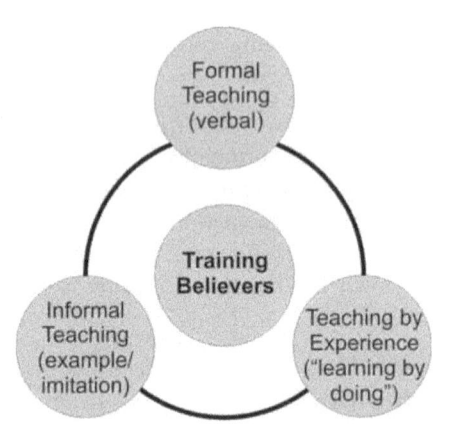

Figure 11: Three dimensions of teaching

Co-workers from a Western background have a tendency to put too much emphasis on the formal side of teaching. However, training through our example and learning by own experiences are equally important for real growth to happen.

Here the basic goals of the training:

- The life as an obedient follower of Jesus Christ by being and sharing Good News.

9. Growing as a Follower of Jesus

- Loving God from all your heart
- Becoming a man or a woman of the Word
- Living a transformed, sanctified life
- Loving others
- Bringing Jesus to others – bringing others to Jesus; to bless his surroundings with Good News
- Training and teaching other new believers.

New believers should understand that they are not only called to accept Jesus' big invitation, but also to glorify God through radical obedience.

Jesus has commanded us to teach everything. However, this does not mean to teach everything at the beginning, or to teach everything at the same time. Teaching is most effective if it is done according to the current needs and not in the order suggested in a course. In the training of new believers, it is very important to "scratch where it itches". We should not see the truth as something which should just be understood, but as something which should be lived out. *Teaching does not have the aim of accumulating knowledge, but of a transformed and sanctified life.*

Not only the sharing of Good News, but also the training of new believers is ideally done in the setting of an oikos, in the context of trusted relationships, where smaller (or also less smaller) groups of believers look together for the application of Scripture and for mutual support in their common walk in obedience to the Word of God.

In Acts, we read about *daily* gatherings (Acts 2:46). Even if this was not possible in your context, a certain regularity and frequency (at least weekly) in your gathering will be important.

Particularly important for new believers from a Muslim background is the transition from a religion based on outward performances to a religion which is based above all on a relationship, of a son to his Father, of a child and not a slave, of faith and not works, of a deep love and not a blind servitude. After this he will also learn that not only his visible acts will be important, but that obedience goes deeper and also includes the thoughts and motives of the heart. The concept of the Holy Spirit living in him will be entirely new to him.

The most effective way of teaching is the *inductive method.* In the inductive method, the real teacher is the Word of God and not a human being. In that way, the new believer learns from the start *to look for solutions to his questions directly in the Scriptures and not from men.*

The following is a very practical way in which this can be done: encourage him to take a notebook and draw three columns:

The Word of God: Write down the verse word by word	*The meaning*: re-write the verse in your own words	*The application*: write down how you will obey each verse
1 Peter 4:10: "Each one should use whatever gift he has received to serve others	Each believer has received some gift from God; the purpose of this gift is to serve others.	I want to be thankful to God for the gifts he has given me. I decide to serve my family and other believers.

Table 10: Example of an inductive Bible study

The inductive method is particularly effective in a group or in a faith community. When each participant has finished writing the three columns on a particular passage or verse, they all come together and share what they have learned and how they will apply it in their lives. The group can then decide together their steps of obedience and faith.

The most important element in training new believers is prayer and intercession. Before, during and after the gatherings: bathe them in prayer! Remember that there is no-one who desires the spiritual development of believers more than the Lord himself.

Baptism matters

Baptism is often viewed as a last and final step of a longer process with many steps and phases. It is a powerful symbol of declaring ones death to the old life, and rising out of the water into a new life and spiritual identity in Christ (Rom 6:3-4). The new believer needs the direction of the Holy Spirit to know when and how he should get baptized.

No doubt, however, New Testament practice was to baptize new believers soon after their conversion to Christ (Acts 2:41; 8:12; 9:18; 16:33). A delayed baptism may cause the new believer to see this as a sign of mistrust in the genuineness of his conversion; certainly not the right way to strengthen his spiritual growth. In some situations it seems wise to wait until several believers can be baptized together, and thus to create an immediate support network.

From experience we know that because baptism is seen as such a decisive step, it is often accompanied by severe difficulties. Therefore, the new believer must be strong enough spiritually (not at the level of time or knowledge but at the level of his commitment and dedication) before being baptized.

9. Growing as a Follower of Jesus

It is not really that important when exactly the baptism takes place. It is more important that the new believer gets regular and adapted teaching and a warm welcome in a culturally integrated house fellowship.

The place of the baptism should be planned carefully. A discreet and half-public place is preferable to a public place. The baptism must not be made public. Ideally, it takes place in the setting of a house fellowship of believers from the same socio-cultural network or even from the same *oikos*. In any case, only a limited group of believers who understand all the implications of baptism for this person should participate, so that unnecessary difficulties or persecutions will not be provoked.

For legal reasons, minors and wives may need the permission of their parents or husbands. By asking for permission, they show that they want to be obedient and remain in the family. If permission is not granted, they will quietly and humbly live out their lives as followers of Jesus by a respectful and pure lifestyle, hoping and waiting until the situation changes.

Many Muslims are polygamous. Should they immediately be accepted for baptism? Some church groups feel that they can only be baptized once they have sent away all their wives but one. We do not want to impose our own norms here, but believe that the Biblical witness does not support such practices. Indeed, nothing should stop a believing polygamist from being baptized. In the ideal scenario, his wives will be baptized with him, and this large *oikos* will become the starting point of a new community of faith. The believing man is encouraged to participate in all activities of the house fellowship, including the Lord's Supper, but he does not qualify to be an elder. There is also the possibility for the sake of the gospel that a man continues to live with only one wife, but cares for the others without disowning them. He will likewise be a testimony to the community by handling this delicate matter in a socially acceptable way.

The communal aspect of baptism must be underlined. Whoever gets baptized is baptized into the body of Christ. The baptized person should understand that all believers are equal in Christ and that all cultural and racial barriers have been brought down (cp. Gal 3:28).

Dealing with spiritual bondage

Sooner or later the question of charms and curses, the hand of Fatima, the evil eye, and other occult practices in Islam, and the glorious freedom in Christ needs to be addressed. A few points that can help us to deal with it:

- *God is light, there is no darkness in him*

    God is good and perfect, there is no evil and no wrong in him: And this is the message which we have heard from Him, and we announce to you: God is light, and no darkness is in Him, none! (1Jn 1:5)

We cannot serve two masters: either we serve God, who is perfect light or we continue serving the darkness and its master who is the devil. God's Word tells us that we should not make any images or any kind of idols besides our God. We also should not put our trust in any kind of occult mechanism to protect us from evil. Our God is a jealous God, no one should put his trust in anything else than God alone!

- *God has conquered all powers of darkness through Jesus Christ*

    And having disarmed the powers and authorities, he made a public spectacle of them, triumphing over them by the cross. (Col 2:15)

All powers and principalities of the darkness were conquered by God through the death of Jesus Christ. Through the Holy Spirit, who lives in us, we are God's children, and because of this we are totally under the protection of the Almighty God. Nobody or nothing can come against us, no evil powers nor curses nor anything else in the visible or invisible world:

    For I am convinced that neither death nor life, neither angels nor demons, neither the present nor the future, neither height nor depth, nor anything else in all creation will be able to separate us from the love of God that is in Christ Jesus our Lord. (Rom 8:38-39)

- *Practical steps that lead to freedom*

    o Confess that you have sinned against God's commandment "you should have no other gods besides me".

    o Receive forgiveness in the Name of Jesus.

    o Turn away from all occult practices.

    o Resist the devil and flee from him.

    o The blood of Jesus sets you free from all bondages.

    o Destroy any kind of charms or idols or anything else that is related to occultism in your life. Follow the early believers in the Book of Acts who were burning all their occult books and got rid of any kind of occultism in their lives:

    Many of those who believed now came and openly confessed their evil deeds. A number who had practiced sorcery, brought their scrolls together and burned them publicly. When they calculated the value of the scrolls, the total came to fifty thousand drachmas (= silver coin, worth one days wage). In this way, the Word of the Lord spread widely and grew in power. (Acts 19: 18-20)

    o Renounce all allegiance to any religious system and spiritual authority other than Christ.

9. Growing as a Follower of Jesus

- o Let Jesus be Lord over all areas in your life and ask God to fill you totally with his Holy Spirit. (see Eph 5:18)

Conclusion: Whoever follows Jesus is protected in the visible and invisible world. Nobody can harm him. People can persecute him, but they can never separate him from the love of God which is in Jesus Christ.

10
Home Based Fellowships of Faith

Home-based fellowships of faith are the natural result of the preceding steps. When followers of Jesus have reached the participation-phase of our cycle, they will meet with other fellow believers, in order to enjoy fellowship and community, to be a "fellowship of faith".

Our aim is not reached when a handful of people, whether few or many, from a particular culture or language, follow Jesus. Our goal is only reached when there are many self-reproducible fellowships of faith in a particular people group.

Three basic activities need continually to take place with three categories of people:

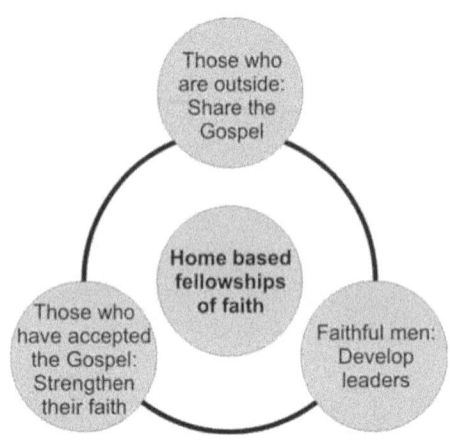

Figure 12: New fellowships of faith: Three basic activities

Biblical Definition

Before speaking about new fellowships of faith, we should be aware of what we should or would like to see. In other words, we need first to work on a Biblical definition. Only then will we be able to determine which forms are recommendable or even possible. The Biblical definition for fellowships of faith brings us back to our starting point: the family. Biblical faith communities are family-oriented: they gather in houses as extended *oikos*.

10. Home Based Fellowships of Faith

- *Jesus often taught in homes*

  As Jesus and his disciples were on their way, he came to a village where a woman named Martha opened her home to him. (Lk 10:38)

  Now one of the Pharisees invited Jesus to have dinner with him, so he went to the Pharisee's house and reclined at the table. (Lk 7:36)

  He came to Jesus at night and said, 'Rabbi, we know you are a teacher from God. For no-one could perform the miraculous signs you are doing if God were not with him.' (Jn 3:2)

- *The apostles often taught in homes*

  Day after day, in the temple courts and from house to house, they never stopped proclaiming the good news that Jesus is the Christ. (Acts 5:42)

- *The first communities of the new faith usually met in the homes of believers*

  The churches in the province of Asia send you greetings. Aquila and Priscilla greet you warmly in the Lord, and so does the church that meets at their house. (1Cor 16:19)

  Give my greetings to the brothers at Laodicea, and to Nympha and the church in her house. (Col 4:15)

  ...To Apphia our sister, to Recipes our fellow-soldier and to the church that meets in your home. (Phm 2)

  Greet also the church that meets at their house. (Rom 16:5a)

- *The New Testament underlines the importance of hospitality*

  Share with God's people who are in need. Practice hospitality. (Rom 12:13)

  Now the overseer must be above reproach, the husband of but one wife, temperate, self-controlled, respectable, hospitable, able to teach... (1Tim 3:2)

Conclusion: Private homes of believers are the ideal, Biblical place for the gatherings of faith communities. It is therefore foundational for every co-worker to have an open home. Open hearts and open homes make a great team! For a house fellowship to be stable and viable, it needs the five following elements:

- Baptized believers
- Believing families
- Spiritually qualified and locally recognized elders
- A meeting place, e.g. a believer who makes his home available for gatherings
- Financial independence and a local ministry of the fellowship to those around them.

The first steps

As soon as the first household or at least the first "person of peace" has accepted Jesus' big invitation, gatherings should take place. Whenever possible, this should happen within the existing social networks of the new believers.

Such communities of faith are not dependent on large numbers. They can easily be started with just two or three members (for example a "man of peace" together with his nuclear family). Jesus promised that where two or three gather in his name, he would be present (Mt 18:20).

It is important to note that often it will not be the co-worker from the outside who actually starts a new fellowship of faith; rather it is the local person of peace. The co-worker from the outside fulfills much more the role of a "midwife" whose work simply is to help the pregnant woman during delivery: s/he shares Good News with a person of peace, invites her/him to follow Jesus, teaches, encourages and accompanies her/him. However, it is the responsibility of this person of peace to draw her/his environment to Jesus by being an exemplary follower of Jesus, by praying much, and then by sharing God News, and leading others to Jesus.

Here are some important principles to follow, during this initial phase of the new community of faith:

- *Work with the entire household/oikos*

Always aim at working with the man of peace *and* his nuclear, or even his extended family and social network. The higher the level of trust that has been established among the followers of Jesus, the stronger, more stable and viable the community of faith will be. If two or three individuals, who did not know each other before, try to meet together as a community, it will always be less solid. When such scattered followers of Jesus are brought together, too often the co-worker from outside is their only point of contact, and when this person no longer works with this group for whatever reason, it will most likely fall apart again.

- *Build around the local person of peace*

If you aim at viable, long-lasting local faith communities, you should not build around you as co-worker from the outside, but from the start around local believers. If ever possible, gatherings should take place in *their* house and under *their* leadership. In the initial phase, you might take on a leadership role, but begin to delegate responsibilities as soon as possible. You will always be the outsider, but they are the insiders in their social circle and they have an easier access to their people. If it is too difficult for them to always exercise hospitality, the meeting place may be changed from time to time.

- *Encourage and model simple and reproducible meetings*

If academic training and the ability to teach for forty minutes are required, nobody apart from you will feel adequate to lead a meeting, and everything will always depend on you. Therefore, *the meetings should be as simple as fits the group, to encourage the man/woman of peace (or other more mature local believers) to assume as much responsibility as possible.* It is advisable to use question-answer style (the inductive method that we introduced in chapter nine). An inductive Bible Study is obedience-oriented and easy to lead - every mature believer can read a text and ask a few questions.

Such simple gatherings contain the following elements (cp. Acts 2:42):

- *Prayer:* confession of sins, worship, intercession, prayer for each other's needs
- *Teaching:* inductive, not preaching style; questions – answers; according to real felt needs
- *Fellowship* around a meal or some tea.
- *The Lord's Supper,* possibly combined with a meal.

- *Aim at a local house fellowship, even if the man of peace is the only follower of Jesus at the moment*

If the person of peace is the only follower of Jesus from his socio-cultural environment, we might be tempted to integrate him into an existing traditional church. However, if you do this, you will lose the potential of implanting a new community of faith into his social network, and thus to bless it with the Gospel. It is therefore much more effective to accompany and encourage this new believer. Further, we can show him how he can work through his network just like yeast through the dough in order to invite others to follow Jesus. This way might be harder, but will bear more fruit on the long run.

Encourage the person of peace to:

- be and share Good News to his social network
- give witness about the hope which he has in him; show him how to do this (simple stories, personal testimonies…)
- have simple, non-aggressive evangelism meetings in his home (films, Old Testament stories)
- understand that the solution is not to cut himself off from his social network by integrating him into an existing church. He should learn to view himself as a bringer of blessing to his family and people, as a multiplier of the gospel, as a planter of a new, culturally sensitive fel-

lowship of faith. Nobody will ever be more ideally positioned to do this than he. Other men of peace such as Cornelius (Acts 10:24) can be an example for him.

It might be useful to note that *from a theological point of view*, nothing speaks against him joining an existing church of a different culture and language. However, *from a strategic point of view*, this would be a sad mistake, since the potential, the ideal key to give birth to new communities of faith in this culture would be lost. In addition to this, experience has shown that in predominantly Islamic regions new believers from a Muslim background often do not feel at ease with, and sometimes even get rejected by Christians from traditional churches. In the end, of course, it is up to the new believer what s/he decides to do, but we can encourage her/him to stay within her/his socio-cultural heritage.

Whenever the person of peace is separated from his/her socio-cultural network, a great opportunity to fulfill God's mandate to bless an entire people has been missed, since we lose the most natural way and ideal bridge of doing it. In this initial phase, all efforts should be made so that he will not jeopardize the good relations with his surroundings. In many instances, this might mean that the new believer will continue to participate in the cultural, social and religious activities of his society. He will perhaps continue to observe some forms of his former religion for a time, in the aim of avoiding an initial rejection by the society.

The following diagram summarizes this initial phase of the new fellowship:

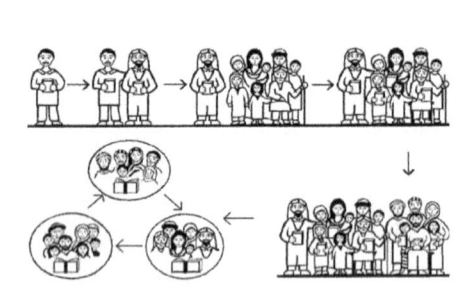

The messenger from the outside established a relationship with the local person of peace. It will be this person of peace rather than the messenger from the outside who will share the biblical message with his *oikos* and invite it to accept Jesus' big invitation. The result will be a first community of faith. When the Gospel is implanted into additional social networks, new house fellowships will start. When there are several such communities, they are in an organic relationship, in a network with each other.

Figure 13: Beginnings and first phases of the fellowship

Ideally, all these activities are done as a team. You, as well as the persons of peace, should work in teams. Ideally, an additional mature local believer can be found who will act as a local co-leader for the emerging fellowships. One harvest worker shares:

> I asked one of my mentors at what stage he had turned over the leadership to the local believers in the house fellowships that he had started. His answer was: „I never did, because I was never leading them!" This principle is called „Shadow pastoring". It means to envision a new believer right from the beginning, and to see in him the potential of a leader for a future house fellowship. The worker is discipling the new believer one to one. However, he does not invite him into any existing house fellowship, but encourages him to share the Good News with friends and family members in order to start soon *his own* house fellowship. The experienced worker does never show up on meetings of this new house fellowship, but he lets the new believer lead it. We saw in our work how the Lord was using new believers, *men and women*, to start new communities of faith through their social networks. As experienced workers we stay during the whole process in the background (or shadow) of these new believers. So, for this reason we never have to turn over leadership, as the community of faith is led by the new believer right from the start.

The community of believers

The body of Christ is made up of people from every race, people group and social class:

> There is neither Jew nor Greek, slave nor free, male nor female, for you are all one in Christ Jesus. (Gal 3:28)

All of the believers, coming from all kinds of backgrounds, form a new community, a new people, the family of God. In spite of this fact, many believers will feel more at ease in a well-known environment: same culture, similar social class, same language, possibly men and women separated etc. Even though they do not meet regularly with believers of other cultures, they understand and emphasize the unity of God's family. They meet within their familiar environment, not for theological, but much more for practical and strategic reasons. In addition, please note that *the main obstacle to most Muslims for not becoming followers of Jesus is rarely of a theological nature, but mostly social and cultural.*

Before a Muslim follows Jesus he will wonder: which group will I belong to if I follow Jesus? It would be a pity, if he did not follow Jesus just for cultural and social reasons. We should therefore "lower" the cultural and social barriers in order to facilitate his acceptance of Jesus' big invitation.

For a new believer, it is crucial to identify himself with a group of like-minded people. This is much more than simply a spiritual home, but also a sense of social belonging. Only a community of believers from a similar background can really offer him just that.

Conclusion: we work within homogeneous groups not for *theological* reasons (since all are one in Christ), but for *strategic* reasons (since it makes it easier for Muslims to accept Jesus' big invitation).

The meeting place

As we discussed already, in New Testament times the natural meeting places for the new disciples were the homes of believers. It is important to realize that during the first 150 years of the Church there were no church buildings. Indeed, there are no sacred buildings or places (pilgrimage sites or holy shrines) in Biblical Christianity. It is the believers themselves who are the temple of the Holy Spirit:

> Do you not know that your body is a temple of the Holy Spirit, who is in you, whom you have received from God? (1Cor 6:19)

Followers of Jesus in a Muslim context normally meet in a contextual place, such as for example in a simple room in the home of one of the believers. Since the word "church" in the biblical sense is defined by "the assembly of those called out" and not by "building", gatherings are possible anywhere. A Somali nomad once put it like this: "As a Muslim, all I need to pray is my mat, and I can pray anywhere. We see you Christians pray once a week, and this in a building. If you can strap your church building to the back of a camel, I will think that the Christian faith is relevant to us Somalis too."

Culturally sensitive faith communities have answers to such challenges because they are highly flexible and adapt easily. To them a nomadic church that meets under a tree or tent is quite suitable; an on-the-road Bible seminary for nomadic people well conceivable; elders without formal theological training administering the Lord's Supper fully permissible; and baptizing people in desert communities through "immersion in sand" absolutely justifiable.

Such communities have learned to discern the substantial from the symbol, the real thing from the shadow. In substantial matters they adhere to biblical principles. In insubstantial matters they are very flexible, always looking for contextual approaches. The following table summarizes the twelve distinct advantages of house fellowships over big church congregations:

Twelve advantages of house fellowships	
Pastoral care	Since the group is small, a member is immediately missed, and can be visited straight away.
Suitable teaching	Since the leaders know the group so well, they can adapt the Biblical teaching to the needs of the group.

10. Home Based Fellowships of Faith

Sense of community	Since all the members know each other well, a sense of community and family is attained naturally.
Not expensive	Since there is no building to keep, or a full-time pastor to pay, costs are much less.
Participation of all	Since the group is small, it needs the gifts of all its members to be able to function.
Help and mutual assistance	The warm atmosphere of a small group encourages the members to give and receive help quickly.
Strong social ties	Since the group sees itself as a family with strong ties, it is less likely for one of the members to stay away or backslide.
Effective evangelism	Unbelievers who would never put a foot inside a church building can accept an invitation to an informal family meeting in the house of a friend.
Rapid growth	A small group has more motivation to invite others in order to grow.
Dynamic multiplication	As soon as the group reaches a certain size, it can divide in two cells.
Resistant to persecution	There is no building which can be destroyed, no full-time pastor that could be targeted, no list by which members could be identified. The house fellowship is more secure and can even continue to multiply under pressure (example of China).
Cultural sensitivity	It is easier for a small group to find consensus on issues such as culturally adapted forms of worship or style of fellowship

Table 11: Twelve advantages of house fellowships

In the New Testament, there were two types of meetings: "cell group" and "celebration" gatherings:

> Day after day, in the temple courts and from house to house, they never stopped teaching and proclaiming the good news that Jesus is the Christ. (Acts 5:42)

- *Cells*: house fellowships: small, familiar, high level of trust.
- *Celebration*: the gathering of all the believers in a town or region.

The goal should not be to "plant" a church building. Rather, we should implant the Gospel seed into a new culture and facilitate its growth and multiplication within that culture.

The meeting time

Although most Christians worldwide go to church on Sundays, there is no explicit biblical command to do so. True, we do find biblical examples of believers gathering on the first day of the week (1Cor 16:2 and others), but although the New Testament urges believers not to abandon gathering, it does not specify a day or time to meet.

> And let us consider how we may spur one another on towards love and good deeds. Let us not give up meeting together, as some are in the habit of doing, but let us encourage one another – and all the more as you see the Day approaching! (Heb 10:24-25)

The early church followed the practice of meeting often. In fact, in the period after Pentecost, they met daily (Acts 2:46). The Colossians were told not to allow anyone to judge them in regard to feast days or Sabbath days (Col 2:16). The believers in Rome were told that there was no agreement among Christians in regard to days:

> One man considers one day more sacred than another; another man considers every day alike. Each one should be fully convinced in his own mind. (Rom 14:5)

As we are well aware Muslims are encouraged to join on Fridays for communal prayers:

> O you who believe! When the call is proclaimed to prayer on Friday (the Day of Assembly), hasten earnestly to the remembrance of Allah, and leave off activity (and traffic): That is best for you if ye but knew! (Surah 62:9)

It is therefore possible for the house fellowship to gather on Fridays, during evening, night, early morning, or any other suitable time. It must be emphasized: it is not important *when* the faith community meets, but *that* it meets. Meeting days and times should be set by the local believers.

The contextualized fellowship of faith

Now we will discuss some more important characteristics of New Testament fellowships and what they could look like in a Muslim environment.

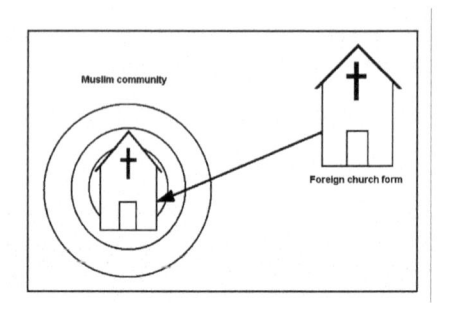

10. Home Based Fellowships of Faith

The principles and practices of the community of faith must have their roots in the New Testament, but at the level of cultural adaptation, the co-workers should be just as flexible as the New Testament is: absolute in regard to dogma, flexible in regard to contextual approaches within a New Testament framework. Simply transplanting a foreign church form as in this drawing would be counter-productive and should be avoided.

Figure 14: Avoid importing foreign church forms into Muslim communities

- *The whole life is worship*

There is no discrepancy between daily life and worship. Not only meetings should be a continuous act of worship, but also our daily life.

> Therefore, I urge you, brothers, in view of God's mercy, to offer your bodies as living sacrifices, holy and pleasing to God – this is your spiritual act of worship. (Rom 12:1)

- *Church is perceived as an organism, not as organization – the Church life is relational, not program-oriented.*

Because a contextual faith community meets in homes, its life focuses on families. A family is not an organization whose members meet formally or weekly. A family is much more an organism whose members are interdependent and whose interactions are informal. Rigid programs are replaced by a loose, informal family atmosphere.

An analysis of the early church shows that common meals were one of the main purposes of their meetings (Acts 2:47; 1Cor 11:33).Common meals were a demonstration of their unity and fellowship as the family of God. In some cultures a treaty is signed or peace is declared with a common meal. When people eat together, they proclaim: We are one family, look, we even eat together!

A joint meal between the members of a house fellowship is the mortar that holds the relationships together; the place where informal counseling, teaching, and encouragement take place. But it is also an opportunity to invite friends and to demonstrate the gospel message by being a hospitable family. In this intimate atmosphere evangelism is very effective. It is easier to invite friends or neighbors to a small group meeting where everyone is noticed than to an impersonal church service. What happens there among the members of the home fellowship, the quality of their lives, their listening, their sharing, their teaching and their prayers, are in themselves evangelistic, even without big preaching and intellectual appeals.

- *Corinthian gatherings: Everyone is involved*

Paul encourages all believers in Corinth to contribute to the meetings according to their gifting:

> What then shall we say, brothers? When you come together, everyone has a hymn, or a word of instruction, a revelation, a tongue or an interpretation. All of these must be done for the strengthening of the church. (1Cor 14:6)

These gatherings are informal. Teaching is done through questions and answers, through an interactive and dynamic teaching method, as everyone is able to participate and obtain the explanations he or she is seeking. All participants actively contribute to the edification of the others: a word of encouragement, a testimony, an exhortation, a prayer, reading a psalm, etc.

- *Naming of Believers*

Just the word "Christian" provokes negative associations for many Muslims, for whom Christianity is often connected with crusades, materialism, moral decay, or American world conquest. To call themselves "Christians" would mean to betray their own culture and people. Even in the Bible, disciples of Jesus are called "Christians" only three times; the first time this happened in Antioch (see Acts 11:26). Much later, more than twenty years after Pentecost, when followers of Jesus were already called "Christians" by some, Paul still referred to himself as a "follower of the Way:"

> I worship the God of our Father as a follower of the Way, which they call a sect" (Acts 24:14a)

The newly established fellowship might therefore search for other, not less biblical, ways to avoid unnecessary barriers: possibly believers could be known as "followers of the Messiah" or just "believers". *As we saw earlier, a Muslim does not have to become a "cultural Christian" in order to follow Jesus!*

- *Prayer forms*

The western church has developed prayer forms that might not defy scriptural teachings, but that are not found in Scripture either, such as praying with closed eyes or folded hands. For a Muslim-born believer these forms may be very alienating, and s/he will therefore look for other, more contextual prayer forms.

With certain key alterations or substitutions, s/he can continue in the familiar pattern of prayer which is valued both by her/him and by her/his Islamic society. In the Old Testament the lifting up of hands toward heaven usually accompanied kneeling or standing (cf. Exod. 9:29; 1Kings 8:22; 2Chron 6:13). This practice was so common that it became a synonym for prayer in Psalm 141:2, 'May my prayer be counted as incense before Thee; the lifting up of my hands as the evening offering.' We conclude that eyes were open during prayer from the statement that the publican would not "lift up his eyes to heaven" (Luke 18:13), and also Jesus Himself in looking up to heaven as He prayed (Mark 6:41; 7:34). The Bible does not speak of praying with eyes closed.

10. Home Based Fellowships of Faith

For believers from a Sufi-oriented background, the most familiar prayer form is the *"Dua"*-style: hands raised to heaven, kneeling or sitting cross-legged, and praying in his heart language. He can pray to God, the creator of heaven and earth, in the name of Jesus the Messiah.

- *Worship style*

While worshipping God is essential, believers in various contexts must find their own cultural expressions of worship. For example, in most Muslim sects, it is not allowed to accompany worship with musical instruments, so verses from the Quran are often recited rhythmically or with intonation.

Adapted forms can be put in place: chanting scripture or creeds rhythmically, reading psalms, or hymns from the New Testament with the intonation of Islamic teachers, declaring a contextual creed such as discussed in chapter 9.

- *Avoiding practices that are culturally unfamiliar*

No social or cultural barrier should exist between the environment and the faith community. It can therefore adopt the following forms:

   o Contextual furniture: on mats and carpets, not on chairs or benches
   o Contextual clothing: ordinary, that is "normal" from the surroundings' viewpoint; without shoes
   o Contextual meeting time: not Sunday morning, but rather on Fridays or another day
   o Contextual framework: Possibly men and women separated

- *The Lord's Supper is celebrated regularly*

According to the command of the Lord ("...do this in remembrance of me", Luke 22:19b), the Lord's Supper is celebrated regularly, often as an integral component of a common meal, following the example of the church in Corinth (1Cor 11: 20-21.33).

- *Leadership is provided by bi-vocational elders (heads of households), not full-time pastors*

As in the Book of Acts, house churches are led by elders, heads of households who usually work as tentmakers. These lay leaders are typically bi-vocational and come from the general profile of the people group.

Leaders of the fellowships meet the biblical qualifications for elders (cf. table 7). They are not expected to have a formal academic theological training. First and foremost they are expected to have a mature and spiritual personality; the gift of teaching; a flawless lifestyle and testimony within the inner circle of the community (family, house fellowship) as well as in the wider circle (tent-maker activity, society); the gift to shepherd and teach other believers.

Elders will be trained on-site using Bible courses adapted to their context, in order to avoid alienating them from their professional and social environment and their family. To ensure multiplication at all times, such house fellowship leaders are not given financial support from the outside. They support themselves through their own tentmaker activities.

It is the local community of faith that has the last word concerning the forms to adopt: They are "the context" for contextualization. The aim is always the same: to eliminate every cultural and social barrier in order to facilitate Muslims to accept Jesus' big invitation and to put new believers at ease in the gatherings. It is their fellowship, not yours, as the co-worker from the outside. It is therefore the local believers which should be comfortable with the cultural forms of the fellowship, not outsiders. In certain areas this might take place like this:

> The believers come together and greet each other in Arabic with the following words: "*Salaam aleykum*", "Peace be upon you". This greeting ceremony can take an extended time. On arrival everybody takes off his shoes and sits on a carpet or mat that covers the floor. The evening starts with a shared dinner, enjoying ample time for fellowship. After the meal Bibles are distributed and somebody reads a text. Bibles are treated with utmost respect, as they have been taught of always honoring the Holy Books. Instead of reading a short passage people often read through a whole book in the Bible, even if that may take the group several months to complete. A good place to start is the Gospel of Luke. After they have read a chapter or part of it, they discuss together what this text might tell them for their daily life. Often people have questions to ask that came up since their last meeting. Together they seek for answers in the Bible.

> In this process discipleship is taking place. After that there usually follows a time of prayer for one another. Worship can be done by reading and reciting a psalm or by singing. Some may have written songs in their own language and these are the preferred choice. Thus the worship is done in a culturally accepted way, so that newcomers feel comfortable when they join the meeting for the first time. Subsequently they might celebrate the Lord's Supper. As somebody reads or recites a suitable text, everybody remembers the death and resurrection of Jesus Christ. Normally different people are leading the Lord's Supper, so that everybody learns by doing. After the Lord's Supper they will often spend a longer time in prayer. People pray in different body positions. Some are sitting, others stand up and lift their hands, others bow down before God, and others just simply stand and pray to God in the name of Jesus. Usually tea is served afterwards, and people sit together discussing how they can follow Jesus in their community. The fellowship continues and sometimes other topics are discussed, depending on what has happened in the village recently. Finally they agree on their next appointment and depart.

The desired outcome of such cell groups is multiplication. For this reason the community of believers is mainly organic and not so much organized. The aim is that every believer should be able to lead such a meeting and through this new leaders are trained on the job.

Sowing the seed

The community of faith will grow to the extent to which all its members participate in the sharing of the Good News. We should particularly encourage...

- *Believers, especially persons of peace, to open their houses* to share Good News with their extended family and social network and to welcome open people with the aim of launching new house fellowships
- *All of the believers to share the Good News.* There are believers who have a particular gift for evangelism, but at the same time, every believer is called to constantly be an authentic witness in his/her social network (and beyond) in and through his/her daily life. The phenomenal growth of the churches in Acts would never have been possible if all the members had not been constantly and joyfully witnessing in their environment.

We have already discussed the importance of very simple gatherings. The same principle applies to the communication of Good News: The methods used should be as simple, multipliable and culturally appropriate as possible, so that every believer will enjoy to participate. The leaders should be models in that. It will be crucial for new believers to be familiar with the basics of apologetics. They should learn how to respond to difficult questions. They should also know some convincing arguments in favour of the Gospel.

Good management

All we have is a gift from the Lord. Since He has given us abundantly, we can also give with joy and generosity:

> Freely you have received, freely give. (Matt 10:8b)
>
> Remember this: Whoever sows sparingly will also reap sparingly, and whoever sows generously will also reap generously. (2Cor 9:6)

The Bible exhorts believers not to be greedy. It is not possessions or money which are a problem, but our love for these things "...the love of money is the root of all kinds of evil" (1Tim 6:9-10). Problems start when money owns us instead of us owning the money, when we are enslaved by it instead of using it as our servant.

All believers need to demonstrate that everything they own belongs to the Lord; this includes our time, talents, gifts, our money, and homes. We are privileged to put these things at the disposal of God and his kingdom. *A deep inner contentment is the "salary" for whoever has learned to give joyfully and generously.*

The new fellowship should never be financed from outside. If it is financed from the outside, its members will no longer have any motivation to give, and in this way they will be deprived of a huge blessing. It is only when the local fellowship finances itself that a sense of ownership can be grasped, and they will practice responsible stewardship.

House fellowships require not much funds, because:

- o The elders are tentmakers and therefore have their own regular income: there is no need to pay salaries.
- o The meetings are held in the houses of the believers: there are no expenses for rent or maintenance of the facilities.
- o The members of the fellowship help each other when the need arises, as it is common in an extended family: No outside fund-raising is required.

The life of the new Ummah

We have already underlined the importance of the social dimension. Believers from a Muslim background are in particular need of a warm, familiar fellowship, like a family or *ummah*. The Bible uses the beautiful images of a family and a people to describe this community of believers.

> Consequently, you are no longer foreigners and aliens, but fellow citizens with God's people and members of God's household. (Eph 2:19)

In this organic fellowship members are closely connected to each other. *They do not just go to church to attend meetings, but they are the church in every area of their lives.* The "one-another" verses of the New Testament describe best how the life and the fellowship of this family should look like. The following table introduces a few of these key characteristics:

Characteristic	Activity	Bible passage
Love	Love one another deeply, from the heart	1Pet. 1: 22
Edification	Build each other up	1Thess 5:11
Exhortation	Admonish one another	Col. 3: 16; Heb10:25
Care	Its parts should have equal concern for each other	1Cor 12: 25

Characteristic	Activity	Bible passage
Submission	Submit to one another	Eph 5: 21
Encouragement	Encourage each other	1Thess 4:18; 5:11
Honor	Honor one another above yourselves	Rom 12:10
Harmony	Live in harmony with one another	Rom 12:16
Inspiration	Spur one another on towards love and good deeds	Heb 10: 24-25
Confession	Confess your sins to each other	Jam 5:16
Intercession	Pray for each other	Jam 5:16
Hospitality	Offer hospitality to one another without grumbling	1Pet 4:9
Grace	Bear with each other (or: Be gracious with each other)	Col 3:13
Forgiveness	Forgive whatever grievances you may have against one another	Col 3:13
Service	Each one should use whatever gift he has received to serve others	1Pet 4:10
Support	Carry each other's burden	Gal 6:2

Table 12: Characteristics of a biblical faith community

Such a community glorifies God and is a strong testimony to the community, a true blessing to any society, an attraction to all those who do not yet follow Jesus. This also protects against division and heresy and enhances true unity. And where authentic believers live together in harmony, there is the blessing of God. (Ps 133:1-3)

Recognize, develop and establish local leaders

New Testament communities of faith were led by local leaders. Different expressions are used to describe their function: bishop, shepherd, elder (Acts 20:17, 28; Titus 1:5, 7). Paul says that the one who aspires to a leadership function within the community of faith aspires "…a noble task." (1Tim 3:1) The leadership of these communities was always collegiate, that is, composed of several mature members. In the Jewish synagogues, there were usually between seven and nine elders. In the churches of the New Testament, no specific number of elders is required, but they are always in a team. In the context of house fellowships, the ideal is probably two to four leaders, so that multiplication by division is possible. The concept of a single, salaried pastor at the head of a fellowship of faith is unknown in the New Testament.

- *The responsibilities of the elders*

The elders assume the general leadership for the community of faith:

- as guides or leaders they serve the flock as a model (1Pet 5:3)
- as shepherds they provide grazing for the flock (Acts 20:28; 1Pet 5:2): they lead it, (Jn 10:3-4), watch over it by protecting it from danger (Acts 20:28-31, Heb 13:17), feed it, that is provide suitable teaching (1Tim 3:2; 5:17), and take care of the sheep, particularly the weak (Acts 20:35, Eze 34:3-5). They also visit the sick and pray for them (James 5:14).
- as stewards (Tit 1:7) they take care of the overall good functioning of the fellowship: this includes financial (Acts 11:30), doctrinal (Acts 15:6, 12, 15) as well as practical issues. They serve in unity, with collegiality, and according to their gifts. They delegate certain tasks to deacons or other members of the fellowship.
- As shepherds they do not only take care of the sheep in their flock, they also look for such sheep which are not yet part of the flock, and do everything to lead them to it.

Not all the elders take care of all the tasks. Rather, the various tasks are taken care of according to the gifts of each leader:

> Each one should use whatever gift he has received to serve others, faithfully administering God's grace in its various forms. (1Pet 4:10)

- *Recognize, develop and establish local leaders – the process*

To recognize, develop and establish local leaders is one of the most vital tasks for the co-worker, since without a mature local leadership there will never really be a sustainable, stable, local faith community. In the New Testament, we do not find local faith communities without local leadership. Pioneers such as Paul, Peter, Timothy or Titus were never church leaders; rather, they recognized, developed and established local leaders. What does this process look like?

- *Pray:* The Lord Himself will show you the people with the potential to be leaders.
- *Model:* Be an example of a Biblical leader.
- *Observe:* Apply the "principle of faithfulness"

> Whoever can be trusted with very little can also be trusted with much, and whoever is dishonest with very little will also be dishonest with much. (Lk 16:10)

10. Home Based Fellowships of Faith

Who is faithful in little things? Who is really progressing in faith, knowledge and sanctification? Who is showing small signs of a potential leader such as a servant heart, love of sharing the Word of God, a life of prayer, loyalty etc.? Who has a good testimony within the community and in the society?

- *Teach*: formally, informally, by experience: (I do it – he watches; we do together; he does it – I watch and give feedback). It is preferable not to take the future leader out of his professional and social context to give him a formal teaching (e.g. Bible college). Following the example of Paul in the book of Acts, it is better to train him where he is, for example through "TEE-courses" (Theological Education by Extension), periodic workshops, or through evening classes.

- *Delegate partially*: The future leader can only learn if he is given opportunities to use and develop his potential. Therefore, it is so important to encourage him to assume certain responsibilities as soon as possible; for example, to lead parts of a gathering, to pray for the sick, to prepare meetings together with other leaders etc.

- *Delegate entirely*: If the potential leader has proven faithful during the partial delegation, full responsibility can be entrusted to him.

- *Install leaders provisionally*: the elders can be dedicated for a trial period, to see how they cope with this new responsibility.

- *Install leaders definitively*: After the definite installation, the co-worker from the outside can move on to new fields, but will still keep a friendly relationship with the local leadership (see chapter 11).

- *Biblical qualifications for leaders*

The Biblical qualifications for deacons are the right standards, not academic qualifications:

> Brothers, choose seven men from among you who are known to be full of the Spirit and wisdom. We will turn this responsibility over to them... (Acts 6:3)

Leaders should be characterized by personal integrity (good testimony), the fullness of the Holy Spirit, and discernment (full of wisdom). This human and spiritual maturity will help them to minister effectively. Luke reports about Stephen, one of the seven chosen deacons:

> Now Stephen, a man full of God's grace and power, did great wonders and miraculous signs among the people. (Acts 6:8)

Mature believers prove their competence through spiritual, moral, emotional and social competence, manage their family well, and demonstrate ministry skills. Therefore, a special emphasis must be put on moral, emotional and social competence. The following table summarizes Paul's requirements for biblical leaders (cp. with 1Tim 3:1-7; Tit 1:5-9; 1Pet 5:1-4).

Area	Characteristics
Spiritual Competence	Holy and disciplined (striving for sanctification); keeps the teachings of the Word of God (is rooted in and loves the Word of God); does not lord over the flock; is not a new believer; serves God freely, eagerly and with dedication, without compulsion; has a clear conscience
Moral & Emotional Competence	Sober; not given to drunkenness; temperate; decent; not a lover of money; not pursuing dishonest gain; under authority; self-controlled; loves the good; honorable/respectable; not deceitful
Managing the family well	Husband of one wife; manages his household well; children are respectful and obedient; has children who follow the Lord and do not live excessively
Social Competence	Has a good reputation with outsiders, so that he will not fall into disgrace and into the devil's trap; is above reproach/blameless; lifestyle of integrity; not violent; mild; not quick-tempered; righteous; hospitable
Ministerial Competence	Able to teach; able to encourage others by sound teaching; able to refute those who oppose sound doctrine; able to shepherd God's flock

Table 13: Characteristics of a mature personality qualifying for leadership

Approaches that inhibit or accelerate growth

The following table and subsequent diagram summarize the essential principles of this chapter:

Inhibiting Growth	Accelerating Growth
Foreign Identity	*Insider Identity*
The gospel is introduced as a foreign religion that is outside the local ethno religious identity.	The gospel is introduced in a way that is compatible with the local ethno-religious identity.
Believers are extracted out of their families into new communities of believers.	The gospel is implanted into family and community networks.
New believers become cultural Christians.	New believers identify themselves as Muslims who follow the Messiah
Extracted Church	*Indigenous Ekklesia*
Believers are gathered into an aggregate	Churches grow within each believer's fam-

10. Home Based Fellowships of Faith

Inhibiting Growth	Accelerating Growth
church that becomes a new community.	ily and community networks.
New believers are often shunned by their families, breaking them apart.	New believers remain in & cultivate their families, even if fellowship with believers is temporarily curtailed.
Gather extracted believers to a time & place and try to form an entirely new community	Implant the gospel so that the leavening church redeems the pre-existing community.
Believers create new communities with other believers and / or expatriates.	Believers transform natural, pre-existing social networks into Jesus-fellowships.
Outside leadership	*Local leadership*
Outsiders provide leadership in new gatherings, and later appoint local leaders "when they are ready."	Outsiders encourage local believers to provide leadership from the beginning, and reinforce the leadership of the family and community networks.
Outsiders lead because local believers do not know and trust each another. Leadership is for mature, Bible school and seminary trained believers only.	Believers provide leadership as their existing networks come to faith. New believers can lead other new believers on-the-job training for new leaders
Each fellowship elects an outside pastor.	Elders are appointed from within the fellowship.
Foreign Forms	*Local Forms*
Churches gravitate toward foreign forms/customs.	Fellowships develop their own forms for community life and worship that fit their culture.
Church meetings are on Sundays and are conducted in foreign ways of "doing church".	Existing patterns of community are redeemed; believers may choose to meet at other times.
Church traditions often carry as much weight as Scripture in determining "how to do church".	Local, cultural patterns are adapted under the uthority of the Bible for the fellowship's forms/customs.
Church uses foreign religious terminology.	Fellowship uses contextual, adapted terminology.
Event-orientation	*Relationship-orientation*
Centered around clergy and buildings – worship is once a week.	Centered around families and homes – meet as often as felt desirable.
People *go to* church.	Families and community *are* the church.
Foreign Dependence	*Local Autonomy*
Approaches are likely to lead to long-	Approaches are locally replicable and sus-

Inhibiting Growth	Accelerating Growth
term dependence on outside resources: Expensive church facilities, seminary training and salaried full-time leaders that the local fellowship is not able to fund.	tainable: house fellowships, on-site training for leaders and by-vocational leaders.
Private, isolated sharing of Good News	*Half-public sharing of Good News*
Private sharing of the gospel leads toward isolated disciples and an extracted church.	Half-public sharing of the gospel in the frame of an oikos leads toward group consensus and a community within the preexisting social network.
Evangelism is difficult because new converts have to join an entirely foreign community.	Evangelism takes place through natural relationships and familiar networks.

Table 14: Approaches that inhibit or accelerate growth

The other important aspect has to do with the kind of believer's we are seeking to plant:

Extracted Believer: Implanted Believer:

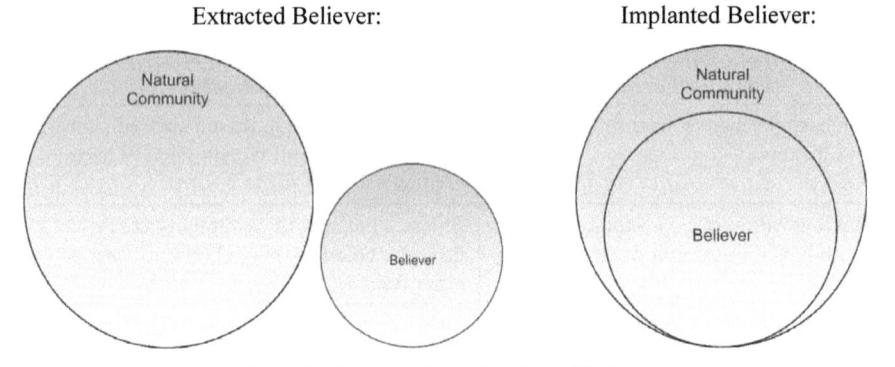

Figure 15: Extracted and implanted believer

When natural and spiritual communities are in competition...
- the family-based community is weakened (sometimes destroyed)
- the spiritual community often has difficulty taking root and growing
- the believer has to manage conflicting identities and dual authority structures

When natural and spiritual communities overlap, they mutually reinforce and strengthen each other.

11
Multiplication

Establish networks of faith communities

Small, isolated house fellowships are in most cases not sustainable. They risk going astray doctrinally, becoming discouraged and wearing out their leadership. We therefore recommend establishing a network of different house fellowships, which in a spirit of humility recognize that they need each other. Some characteristics of such a network:

- *Fellowship among the leaders: the elders* of different communities meet regularly (for example once a month) to encourage each other, share their concerns, mutually advise each other and pray for one other.

- *Celebration*: all the house fellowships in an area or town meet regularly for worship. It is important to combine the two basic types of gathering: the cell (small number, family atmosphere, pastoral care) and the celebration (large number, encouragement). We see in Acts 5:42 that the believers in Jerusalem met in the temple (celebration) as well as in houses (cell).

- *Ministerial gifts:* as the ministerial gifts begin to develop within the house fellowships, they are put into the service of the whole body. A small, single house fellowship may not have all needed ministerial gifts; it therefore needs the enlarged body of Christ in a region or in a town (e.g. giving systematic teaching, counseling, training people for work among children and youth).

- *Joined projects*: A network can realize projects that would be too much for a single fellowship. Examples for such project's are the sending of new co-workers to other regions, offerings for the poor and disabled or holding special workshops and training seminars.

Every community of believers is linked to other communities and thus forming a network. Communities of believers are often not led by elders but by people who have opened their house for meetings. Elders are usually responsible for a network of communities. They visit every single community or at least they meet with their leaders. In this way every leader of a community is under the leadership of a number of elders and is accountable to them.

Through this kind of structure the elders should be free to invest into new leaders and to give vision for the whole network of communities. In doing this they follow the example of Acts 6 where the elders created a structure where they could concentrate on the word and prayer. The bigger the network is, the more elders are appointed. It is possible for a network to split into two networks, and for different elders to be responsible for each network. If at all possible, the different communities of a network should meet regularly, for example once a month, for a larger celebration. For security reasons, such celebrations cannot be done in some Islamic countries.

All the networks, as well as the individual communities, have the aim to multiply. Through the multiplication of networks, and through constant multiplication of communities, we can see a whole people group reached with the Gospel.

Multiplying the community of faith

Our aim is not just a single house fellowship, but rather to bless a whole people group. Every living being, if in good health, grows and multiplies (nature, man). Healthy communities of faith will also grow and multiply. Remember: they are not dead organizations, but living organisms. Here are a few helpful steps towards the reproduction of faith communities:

- *Appropriate teaching and lots of prayer*

All outside co-workers and local leaders should be aware that the fellowship is called to multiply. Teaching in this regard should be given. The whole community should fervently pray and fast for growth and multiplication.

- *Lots of evangelism*

All outside co-workers, local leaders and members of the fellowships should be engaged in sharing the Good News. They will apply the various principles, approaches and methods presented in this book.

- *Practical strategies for multiplication*

Once the community has reached a certain size and is lead by at least two elders it can be divided. The aim is not vertical growth (an ever larger number of believers in one fellowship), but horizontal growth (multiplication of new house fellowships). According to the situation, a group of 10-12 adult members could think and pray about dividing into two fellowships.

> o The members of the fellowship identify new persons of peace within their existing social network. Instead of adding them to the existing faith community, they begin meetings directly in their houses, within their *oikos*, and their social network, with the aim of establishing new house fellowships.

11. Multiplication

- The community of faith sows the seed by using various means of sharing the Good News. New persons of peace start new fellowships in their homes or in the home of one of the older believers.

- *Leadership*

Multiplication can happen through the outside co-workers; however, it is preferable that it happens through the members or the elders of the local faith community. Outside co-workers should always make the effort to implant the Gospel seed into a new *oikos*. The same applies for the members of the local faith community, too. The basic principle is: the more responsibility the local faith community assumes, the better it is.

Transferring leadership

Paul had confidence in the Holy Spirit. He knew that the new fellowships would pass through difficulties. But his physical presence was not necessary to help them through these trials. He counted on the promises of God (Phil 1:6), and was therefore able to leave the churches after a short time and to go further towards new areas (cf. Rom 15:18-24).

According to the situation, he left the work in the hands of the local elders, who served within the fellowships and went on to bless the remaining regions of their area (1Thess 1:8); or he delegated to a faithful co-worker the responsibility of continuing the work by establishing local leadership:

> The reason I left you in Crete was that you might straighten out what was left unfinished and appoint elders in every town, as I directed you. (Tit 1:5)

Before leaving an area, it is absolutely crucial for the co-workers to prepare and train new leaders for the work. The following steps are recommended for the transfer of leadership:

- *Fasting and prayer* (Acts 14:23)
- *Laying on of hands* as a sign of blessing, passing the baton, anointing.
- *Officially recognizing the new leadership.* All members of the network of faith communities should officially know who has the spiritual authority to lead.
- Commend the new leaders to the Lord.

Handing over leadership is always an act of faith. Paul knew about the risk of unfaithful leaders (2Tim 4:10), backsliding believers, and heretic churches (Gal 3:1). In spite of these dangers, Paul dared to transmit the leadership and to move on. The founder or former leader will probably worry about the continuation of the work. However, he must learn to count on the grace of God and the help of the Holy Spirit. His ministry will continue in prayer and intercession. God does not depend on a leader with a lot of experience to continue his work (cf. Moses – Joshua). Men come and go, but the Holy Spirit is always the same. And *sometimes the old leader must fully leave his position before the new leader has all the anointing and authority for his ministry (cf. Elijah – Elisha).*

Finishing well

A good strategy also includes finishing well. Pioneers can leave too early. However, they can also stay too long. *Both leaving too early and staying too long will hinder the good progress of the work and can cause damage.* Coworkers who are particularly gifted to pioneer a work are usually not the best to consolidate or to run it long term. They often have to move on so that the work they pioneered can develop better. This takes special grace for such dedicated workers, and sometimes the shocking realization: if I don't move on now, I will destroy the very work I have built up! The task of the pioneer in a given locality is always temporary, while that of the local people is permanent.

For all these reasons it is of crucial importance that we concentrate from the beginning on the task of recognizing, developing and establishing local leaders. Actually, we should aim at becoming obsolete, following Paul's example who shared the Good News, brought local faith communities to birth, trained and established local leaders, finished well and moved on (cp. Acts 14:21-24).

Epilogue

"...And you shall be a blessing." Whoever you are, wherever you are – if you are an authentic follower of Jesus Christ, you are called to bless other people and particularly people from other cultures and religions.

In this book, we presented to you a wealth of concepts and principles. We have entrusted these to you to implement them by God's grace in your context. This will demand courage, boldness and perseverance. The first steps will be particularly important, but also more difficult.

Jesus never promised an easy life – actually quite the opposite, as we discussed in chapter four. The challenges are numerous, the difficulties might sometimes seem impossible to overcome.

Jesus did promise, however, as we obey and go, to be with us always, to the very end of the age. His presence and his peace will guide you. Trust in him, and, by faith in him and in his help, take the first steps. He will neither disappoint nor forsake you.

The divine mandate to bless all families on earth is not an impossible task. Remember: this mandate is not first of all a heavy command, but a glorious promise. In our generation, more people from a Muslim background have started to follow Jesus than in the entire history before. Within the last three decades, more communities of faith have been planted in Islamic cultures and peoples than ever before. Even within the last few years we have had the privilege to hear about certain Muslim areas where whole villages with hundreds, if not thousands, of people have started to love and obey Jesus the Messiah.

God is fulfilling his promise and blesses all peoples on earth. Even in places where we did not ever expect him to do so.

God invites you today to become part of his worldwide plan to bless all peoples. We hope and pray that your response to this invitation will be a radical 'Yes' and a commitment without compromise.

Appendix 1:
The Straight Path – an Example of a Contextual Approach to Evangelism

(Free download from: http://engaging-with-islam.info/leaflets/Camel_Training_Track.pdf)

I am grateful to King Fahd of Saudi Arabia, Islamic Foundation, and others who have pledged to translate the Arabic Qur'an into all the languages of the world. I am happy that I can now read the Qur'an in my mother tongue. Since less than 20 percent of Muslims around the world can read Arabic most Muslims cannot understand the Qur'an in the Arabic language and must rely on someone else to explain its message to them. In other words, they hear the messages in the Qur'an through the words of another. Increasingly, thanks to King Fahd, this is no longer necessary.

Allah wants you to understand His message, but how can you obey Him if you do not clearly understand what Allah says? Muslims living before the Prophet Muhammad understood what Allah said because Allah spoke to them in their own language. The following story illustrates the importance of understanding Allah's message.

An Arab owner of a garment factory in India wrote a letter in Arabic to the factory workers telling them that they should stop making red shirts and start making yellow shirts. The letter went on to say that the laborers would receive a bonus at the end of the month if they worked hard. The Arab owner spoke neither Urdu nor Hindi, but relied on his office manager who spoke Arabic, Urdu and Hindi. The Indian office manager read the letter out loud *in Arabic* to the factor workers and then placed the letter on a table in front of them. The laborers were happy to receive a letter from the owner, but did not change from making red shirts to yellow ones, because they did not understand his instructions. When the factory owner learned that his factory was still producing red shirts, he was very upset with the manager and with the workers. He decided to hire a new factory manager and all new workers. The Arab owner determined to employ only people who could clearly understand his orders. For if they do as he commands, he is happy to bless them with good pay and bonuses.

Do not miss out on Allah's message. Do not rely on someone else to tell you the message of Allah. Instead, find a Qur'an translated into your own language and together let's discover in it a treasure that will change your life.

Pakka (True) Muslims – Al-Imran 3:42-55

As I was reading the Qur'an in my mother tongue, I came upon a passage that filled my heart with hope. You too can experience this same hope after you receive the Truth found in surah al-Imran 3:42-55. It grieves me to know that not everyone has the eyes to see this Truth. I pray that Allah will open your eyes to recognize His Truth.

> In surah al-Maidah 5:83 we read: "And when **they** listen to what has been sent down to the messenger, you see their eyes overflowing with tears because of the Truth they have recognized. They say; "Our Lord! We believe; so write us down among the witnesses."

Who are the "they" in this *ayyah* (verse)? Who are the people that are able to recognize Allah's Truth? We will find the answer in surah al-Imran. I have read surah al-Imran 3:42-55 countless times. Each time, I feel the same joy that I received the first time I discovered the Truth in this passage. The discovery I made is nothing new. Many people in history have made the same discovery because their eyes were also opened to the Truth. Each day, hundreds of our Muslim brothers' eyes are being opened by Allah as they read surah al-Imran 3:42-55. Those who understand this Truth call themselves "Pakka (True)" or "Complete" Muslims.

Allah is confirming the Truth of al-Imran 3:42-55 by speaking to many Muslims through dreams. A recent survey was conducted of 600 "Pakka Muslims". Out of 600, 150 said that they became "Pakka Muslims" through a dream where a messenger of Allah appeared to them and confirmed the Truth of surah al-Imran 3:42-55. Some "Pakka Muslims" have had dreams where they saw and heard the Prophet Muhammad, peace be upon him, confirm the Truth that is presented in this

booklet. In one of the holy kitabs (books of the Bible written before the Qur'an), an *ayyah* says, "You shall know the Truth, and the Truth shall make you free." Do you want to know the Truth and be set free? Please take the time to open your Qur'an and read for yourself, *ayyah* by *ayyah*, this wonderful passage, surah al-Imran 3:42- 55. I have provided you with my explanation of each *ayyah*. I pray that your eyes will be opened and you will understand this Truth and join the Pakka Muslim movement.

Surah al-Imran 3:42-55 – With Explanation

> **3:42** And (remember) when the angels said: "O Maryam! Verily, Allah has chosen you, and made you pure, and has preferred you above the women of the creation. **3:43** O Maryam! "Be obedient to your Lord and bow with those who bow (in worship).

Before the Injil Sharif (Gospel) was written, there was a period of 400 years in which the people of the Scripture did not have a prophet to speak to them. Allah's people had reached the bottom of the pit of despair and hopelessness. It was at this dark moment in the history of the world, that

Allah did something very unusual. He spoke through the angel Jibreel to a young virgin named, Maryam. The angel told her that Allah chose her for a special assignment. But first, Maryam was to reaffirm her calling as a true Muslim. She was told to totally submit herself in obedience to Allah.

> **3:44** This is of the tidings of things hidden. We reveal it unto you. You were not present with them when they threw their pens (to know) which of them should be the guardian of Maryam, nor were you present with them when they quarreled thereupon.

The story behind ayyah 44 is not clear. It seems that the religious leaders called several young bachelors together. Once they were assembled, they cast lots to see which of them would be chosen by Allah for this noble cause of caring for Maryam and her baby. History tells us that Joseph became the husband of Maryam.

In no other place in the Qur'an do we read of this much excitement taking place in heaven. Allah was about to do something very special for all the people of the world; something that has never been done before or since.

> **3:45** (And remember) when the angels said: "O Maryam! Verily, Allah gives you the glad tidings of a Word from Him, whose name Isa Masih (Jesus Messiah), the son of Maryam, held in honor in this world and in the Hereafter, and one of those brought near to Allah."

Ayyah (verse) 45 is the announcement to Maryam that she had been chosen to give birth to the prophet Isa. Muslims around the world have two names for Isa. They call him "Isa Kalimatullah" (Isa the Word of Allah) and "Isa Ruhullah" (Isa the Spirit of Allah). Why do Muslims call Isa by these two names?

The answers are found in surah al-Imran 3:45 and surah Ambiyaa 21:91. Allah said that He would put his Word into Maryam. What or who is Allah's "Word?" To better understand this, read surah Ambiyaa 21:91 "…and she (Maryam) guarded her chastity, therefore We breathed into her of our Spirit and made her and her son a sign for all people." Why do we refer to Isa as "Isa Kalimatullah" and "Isa Ruhullah?" The Qur'an makes it clear; Isa is the Word (Kalim) and Spirit (Ruh) of Allah. No other person or prophet carries these titles.

Allah's "Word" and "Spirit" were placed inside of Maryam and became a living baby. Allah told Maryam to name the baby Isa al-Masih (Jesus the Messiah). Al-Masih means "the anointed or promised one." 758 years before the

Appendix 1

birth of Isa, the prophet Isaiah wrote, "...a virgin will conceive and his name will be called, 'Immanuel' (Isaiah 7:14). "Immanuel" is a Hebrew word meaning, "Allah is with us." Isa would be honored by all people in this world and forever in heaven and he would be one of those nearest to Allah Himself.

The Qur'an paints a picture of Isa for us. He is Allah's Kalim (Word), His Ruh (Spirit), (al-Masih) the promised anointed one, and "a sign for (all) the nations" (Ambiyaa 21:91). When we want to go somewhere that we have never gone before, we look for a sign to guide us. Where will we go if we follow Isa?

> **3:46** "He will speak to the people in the cradle and in manhood, and he will be one of the righteous."

Isa's birth was to be a message to the entire world and he was to be one of the righteous. How righteous was Isa? Allah told Maryam, in surah Maryam 19:19, that Isa would be "a faultless son." The Injil Sharif teaches us that Isa never killed anyone; he did not have a love for money; he never married; he spoke out against corruption among the religious leaders; he prayed every day; he fasted for 40 days and nights in which he did not eat anything at all; and he taught us to love our enemies. If Isa ever committed a sin, then he would have ceased to be Allah's Kalimatullah or Ruhullah and he could not have gone to heaven to be with Allah. Through Isa, Allah showed the world how "Pakka Muslims" should live their lives. This would be a wonderful world if we all lived our lives like Isa.

> **3:47** She said: "O my Lord! How shall I have a son when no man has touched me?" He said: "So (it will be) for Allah creates what He wills. When He has decreed something, He says to it only: "Be!" and it is.

Maryam was shocked at the news that Allah gave her. She said to Allah, "How can I have a baby when I am not married and no man has ever touched me?" Allah was very patient with Maryam. He answered her, "I am Allah; it is easy for me to do what I wish."

Knowing that Allah does nothing by accident, all that Allah does is according to his perfect plan, **why would Allah have Isa born without a father?** Has there ever been another prophet born without a father? What does this event mean to all Muslims?" To answer these questions we must look closely at the life of Adam. In al-Imran 3:59, the Qur'an says that Isa is like Adam. They were similar because both of them had no earthly father. Before Adam disobeyed Allah, he walked with Allah in the garden (paradise). Adam could live in Allah's presence forever and talk to Allah because he did not have any sin, just like Isa. Adam, at first, was righteous and holy because he was created that way by Allah and filled with Allah's holy breath. Once Adam disobeyed Allah, Adam became unholy and could no longer live with Allah in the garden (paradise). Read in the Qur'an 20:121:

"Then they (Adam and his wife) both ate of it, so their shame became apparent unto them, and they began to hide by heaping on themselves some of the leaves of the garden, and **Adam disobeyed** his Lord and his nature became evil."

Most certainly, all of us are children of Adam except one – his name is Isa al-Masih. Apple trees produce only apples! Can an apple tree produce oranges? All humans born in Adam's family inherit Adam's nature. The curse of sin in Adam is being passed down among his descendants. Isa is the only man who never sinned. He did not sin because he was not born in the blood line of Adam. He did not inherit Adam's sinful nature. Now do you understand why I love to read the Qur'an? Because it show us that Isa is the Word and Spirit of Allah, that he was the anointed promised one, and that he was sinless! All of this has enlightened me. But wait, there is more…

> **3:48** And He (Allah) will teach him the Scripture and wisdom, and the Taurat (Torah) and the Injil (Gospel).

Allah taught Isa the holy Kitabs (Sacred Scriptures). Pakka Muslims read and understand **all** four Kitabs: the Taurat, the Zabur, the Injil, and the Qur'an. Allah instructed Muhammad, peace be on him, that if he had a question about any message from heaven, that he should look for the answer among those who read the "Before Kitabs", i.e. those Kitabs written before the Qur'an.

> Surah Yunnus 10:94 says "And if thou (Muhammad) art in doubt concerning that which We reveal unto thee, then question those who read the Scripture (that was) before thee. Verily the Truth from thy Lord hath come unto thee. So be not thou of the waverers."

I have read the Taurat (Torah), the Zabur (Writings), and the Injil (Gospels). These Kitabs have been translated directly from the original languages and are trustworthy. A friend of mine said that reading the "Before Kitabs" makes him feel like a **Complete** Muslim. A cow with only one leg cannot stand, but when he stands on all four legs, he is strong. A "Pakka Muslim" reads all of the Kitabs.

> Surah 4:136 "O ye who believe! Believe in Allah and His messenger and the Scripture which He hath revealed unto His messenger, and the Scripture which He revealed aforetime. Whoso disbelieveth in Allah and His angels and His scriptures and His messengers and the Last Day, he verily hath wandered far astray."

Have the "Before Kitabs" been changed? The Qur'an says, "No!" Is Allah not powerful enough to protect His message? Read in the Qur'an surah an-An'am 6:115-116

> "Those unto whom We gave the Scripture (aforetime) know that it is revealed from thy Lord in truth. So be not thou (O Muhammad) of the waverers. Perfected is the Word of the Lord in truth and justice. **There is no one that can change His words.** He is the Hearer, the Knower."

No one can change the words of Allah. If someone tells you that the "Before Kitabs" have been changed, ask them, "Who changed them and when were they changed?" Then ask them, "Why does the Qur'an which was written 600 years after the Injil, not tell us that the Injil has been changed?" Now read

> al-Imran 3:49 And will make him (Isa) a messenger to the Children of Israel (saying): "Lo I come to you with a sign from your Lord. Lo! I fashion for you out of clay the likeness of a bird, and breathe into it, and it is a bird by Allah's leave; and I heal him who was born blind, and the leper, and I raise the dead, by Allah's leave. And I announce to you what you eat, and what you store up in your houses. Lo! herein is a sign for you, if you are to be believers.

When I first read this story of Isa making a live bird out of clay, I thought back to the story of how Allah had also created Adam out of the dirt of the ground. According to the Qur'an, ayyah 49, Allah gave Isa the power to create life. With the power of Allah, Isa also healed lepers, the blind, the crippled, and even raised the **DEAD TO LIFE**. After reading this *ayyah*, once again my soul is filled with hope. Isa has been given power over life and death. POWER OVER DEATH, this is amazing! Before, I had thought that death was my greatest enemy in the world. But now I realize from the Qur'an that Isa was given power over death. The world has been waiting for someone who can conquer our greatest and final enemy, death. If Isa was given the power of life and death, what can he do for us?

> **3:50** And I have come confirming that which was before me of the Taurat (Torah), and to make lawful some of that which was forbidden unto you. I come unto you with a sign from your Lord, so keep your duty to Allah and obey me.

Isa said that his life verified or confirmed what the prophets had spoken about him in the 'Before Kitabs.' The old prophets spoke much about Isa al-Masih. When I read the "Before Kitabs," that have been translated from the original languages, I found over 300 prophesies (foretelling) about Isa! In al-Imran 3:50 Isa tells us that our duty to Allah is to obey him (Isa)! To show your highest respect to Allah, you must obey Isa. The only command of Isa that we find in the Qur'an is here in 3:50. The command is clear, "Obey me" (Isa). Later you will see an amazing promise of a blessing given to those who obey the commands of Isa.

If we are to obey the commands of Isa, where can we find these commands? They are found in the Injil. How can you do your duty to Allah and obey Isa unless you know what he has commanded you to do? You must find out what the Injil says so that you can know how to obey Isa? The same Injil that Muhammed, peace be upon him, used is available today. When you find an Injil, be sure to check to see if it was translated from the original Greek language in which it was written in the 1st century.

3:51 Truly! Allah is my Lord and your Lord, so worship Him. This is the Straight Path.

A road or path always leads us to something or someone. The Straight Path (Tarika) mentioned in this *ayyah* is the road that leads us to Allah. It is a straight and direct road to Allah. There are no bypasses or turns. It is a direct path which means that it does not stop short of its intended goal which is heaven. So who can travel on this path to Allah? Have you ever heard someone say, "If I do enough good works, Allah will let me go to be with Him in heaven after I die?" The one who says this is blind and insults the holiness of Allah. No matter how many good works you do, you can never remove the fact that your life also includes times when you have disobeyed Allah.

Allah is 100 percent holy and no sin can come into His presence. Remember that Adam was removed from the presence of Allah because of his one sin. 99.9 percent holy people cannot go to heaven. In fact there is no such thing as 99.9 percent holiness; holiness is always 100 percent. Only people who have their sins removed from them can go to be with Allah. This is sad news for us, because we have all sinned. Our only hope is that Allah will create a way for us to be totally cleansed of our sin and our sinful nature.

3:52 But when Isa came to know of their disbelief, he said: "Who will be my helpers in the cause of Allah?" The disciples said: "We will be Allah's helpers. We believe in Allah, and bear witness that we are muslims (i.e. we submit to Allah)." **3:53** Our Lord! We believe in that which You have sent down, and we follow him that You have sent (Isa). Enroll us among those who witness (to the Truth)

In order to get all of the people of the world to worship Allah alone, Isa asked for some helpers. A small group of men came forward saying that they are Muslims and that they will help Isa. They said that they believe in Allah's message and the messenger (Isa) that He sent down. According to the Qur'an, the followers of Isa are Muslims! Nowhere in the Qur'an does it say that Muslims are released from their responsibility to follow Isa. The Qur'an never says that one prophet cancels out the authority of another prophet!

3:54 And they (disbelievers) schemed (to kill Isa) and Allah schemed too: and Allah is the best of the schemers.

Satan hates Truth and will do everything he can to make sure that people do not hear it. How long have you been reading the Qur'an and yet you have never understood surah al-Imran 3:42-55? Satan does not mind if you can **read** the Qur'an, but he does have a great concern if you **understand** the Qur'an. Allah will not allow Satan to win. He has a plan to give Truth to all the people in the world.

There were two plans for the death of Isa. The leaders of the Jews had a plan to kill Isa and Allah had a plan for the death of Isa. Does the Qur'an ever say

Appendix 1

that Isa did not die? No. Surah The Women 4:157 says that the Jews said that they did not kill or crucify him. Note that the *ayyah* does not say "Isa did not die." Also note that the Jews were not allowed to put anyone to death, only the Romans could do this. So it was actually not the Jews but the Romans who executed Jesus. If you think that the Qur'an says that Isa did not die, read the next *ayyah*.

> **3:55** And (remember) when Allah said: "O Isa (Jesus)! I will *take you** and raise you to Myself and clear you of those who disbelieve, and I will make those who follow you superior to those who disbelieve till the Day of Resurrection. Then you will return to Me and I will judge between you in the matters in which you used to dispute."

Ask your Imam to read in Arabic *ayyah* 55. Listen carefully as he reads. You will hear him say the Arabic word, *"mutawaffika." The root of this word is "tawaffa." This word means "to die" or "to cause one to die." The word, "tawaffa" is used 26 times in the Qur'an. 24 times it is translated, "to die" or "to cause to die." Twice it is translated, "to sleep." Never is it translated, "to take." Translators must be careful to accurately translate the Qur'an into other languages. Therefore, *ayyah* 55 should be correctly translated to say, "And when Allah said: 'O Isa! I will cause you to die and then raise you to Myself...'" Surah Maryam 19:33 Isa says about himself, "Blessed was the day I was born, blessed was the day I died, and blessed was the day I was resurrected." Resurrected means, "raised from the dead." This was Allah's perfect plan. But why would Allah have Isa killed? I will answer this later.

Where is Isa at this time? Ayyah 55 proclaims that Isa was raised up to Allah himself. Remember that Allah is 100 percent holy. If someone is brought directly to Allah, they too must be 100 percent holy as well. No evil or sinful person can come into the presence of Allah. The summary of Isa's life is as follows:

- Born without inheriting Adam's evil nature
- Lived a holy and sinless life
- Allah gave him power over life and death
- Isa traveled the straight path (Tarika) to Allah
- Isa is now with Allah

This is the Truth that comes directly to us from the Qur'an. Pakka Muslims understand this Truth. In the Injil Sharif, Isa made a bold statement about himself. He said, "I am the Way, the Truth, and the Life." (Yuhonna 14:6) Surah al-Imran 3:42-55 agrees with the Injil Sharif. Isa knows the way to Allah because he has traveled the Straight path (Tarika) to Allah. "Isa is the Truth because he is the Word of Allah. Allah's Word is always true. Isa is the Life because he was given power over death.

The Straight Path (Tarika) to Heaven

Blind people need help in traveling. Until I read surah Al Imran 3:42-55, I felt that I was a "spiritually" blind person. My evil and sinful nature prevented me from seeing the straight path Tarika) to heaven. I needed someone to help me. I needed someone who knows the way. Another blind person is of no use to me. It must be someone who has traveled the straight path (Tarika) before and whose home is heaven. Can Isa help us get to heaven? I believe surah al-Imran 3:42- 55 is a special message from Allah. This wonderful message tells about a prophet that came from heaven, lived as a man and then went back to home in heaven. Yes, I believe Isa can help us. At the beginning of this booklet, I presented to you an *ayah* from the Qur'an and then I asked you a question. It is now time to answer that question.

Surah Al Maidah (5:83) "And when **they** listen to what has been sent down to the messenger, you see their eyes overflowing with tears because of the Truth they have recognized. They say; "Our Lord! We believe; so write us down among the witnesses." I asked the question, "Who is the **"they"** in this *ayah*?" The answer is, "The followers of Isa who are called 'Pakka (True)' or 'Complete' Muslims."

How You Can Follow Isa to Heaven

Allah loves you and wants you to be with Him in heaven after you die. But to go to heaven, your sins must be totally removed from you. To fix this problem, Allah developed a way that we could be totally forgiven and the curse of sin removed from us. Starting with Adam, man could be forgiven of his sins if he followed the sacrifice system called *"korban* (sacrifice)." With his sins forgiven and removed, he could join Allah in heaven directly after death.

The *korban* is a picture of the punishment that we deserve for our sins. Think of a court room where you stand before the judge. The judge is fair and just. Because of your sin, the judge sentences you to be killed. Even though you are guilty, Allah allows another person, one who is innocent, to receive your punishment. For Allah to throw away your punishment would mean that he is not a just judge. Every crime must be paid for, this is justice. You deserve to die for your guilt of sin. Think about the Muslim *festival of korban*. First, we are to find a pure animal. A sick or low quality animal cannot be used for the sacrifice. Immediately before the sacrifice, we are to pray to Allah saying, "Allah, I am guilty of committing sin against you. I deserve to have my blood poured out of me until I die. So Allah, please have mercy on me and instead of taking my blood, take the blood of this innocent animal."

From the time of Adam until the time of Isa, *korban* was practiced. Allah did not always require the blood of animals to be used for the *korban*. Ibrahim was told to do the *korban* with his promised son. At the last moment, Allah stopped Ibrahim from sacrificing his son. Allah was only testing Ibrahim's love and devotion to Him.

Pakka Muslims have the clearest understanding of *korban* because they have read all four kitabs. They know that the Muslim followers of Isa stopped practicing the *korban*. Why? Pakka Muslims know that the *korban* was only a shadow of the ultimate *korban*, the *korban* described in al-Imran 3:54-55, that Allah would provide for all the people of the world: past, present, and future. For Allah to do *korban* for all of mankind shows us how much He loves us and gives us confidence that we can be totally cleared of the curse of sin. But what would Allah use for His *korban* for all the people of the world? The Qur'an says that the birth of Isa would be a sign for the world. In order for Allah to do *korban* for all mankind, he needed the most pure, holy, and powerful sacrifice available.

We have seen from the Qur'an that the purest, holiest, and most powerful blood in the world was that of Isa. Allah performed the *korban* using the innocent and holy blood of Isa. What Allah prevented Ibrahim from doing with his promised son, Allah Himself did for us with Isa. This was an act of love unlike any we have ever seen, the innocent giving his blood for the guilty. Isa took upon himself the punishment that we deserve. Now you know why Pakka Muslims are such grateful people. They understand that Allah did not give us what we deserve. The Injil says in surah Yuhonna 15:13, "Greater love has no one than this, that he lay down his life for his friends." Isa laid down his life for us.

Today you, too, can become a Pakka Muslim. All you have to do is to believe that Allah gave the *korban* for you, substituting Isa for you. Stop now, hold your hands up before you, and humbly tell Allah that you receive His *korban* and thank Him for placing on Isa the punishment for your guilt and sins. In this way, Allah will forgive you of your sin and remove its curse from you. When you are cleansed of your sins, then you can go to be with Allah after you die. You can now live your life in peace knowing that after death, you can go directly to be with Allah.

This testimony was recreated from the experiences of numerous Pakka Muslims from across the Muslim world.

Appendix 2:
A Short Story for Your Muslim Neighbors

With full respect and love in the service of all who love Islam. Hello friend, I have an amazing story. It takes only five minutes and you will be happy to know it is absolutely free. Would you like to hear my story? At any time you can stop me if you wish not to hear more. First I want to ask you a question. What year is it? 2011, that's good, but do you know why it is 2011? Ok, I'll let you in on the truth. It is 2011 because 2011 years ago they stopped the date and started over. Why? Because a wonderful thing happened then. *(Draw a line from 2011 to 0)* By the way I am telling you this story from information I have gained from the ancient scriptures. You may recognize some of it. The wonderful thing is that 2011 years ago Allah moved according to His plan as our merciful benefactor to solve our greatest problem. We all have sinned and have a dirty left shoulder. Allah loves us and we must be clean to join Him in heaven. We can never erase the wrong we have done, but He can. He sent His Word down from heaven to a young woman and He became a child. Hazrat Isa grew up to be a wonderful Prophet and Savior. He did many wonderful things, but the best thing He did was to perfectly cover our sin and open the door to heaven. That is the wonderful reason the date was changed. It is sad for Him to see so few coming to heaven; that is why I am telling you this story. Are you with me so far? The story begins in the garden at the beginning of man on earth. Adam was formed from the dust and Ewa was formed from a rib from Adam's side. They had all they needed. They saw the fruit Allah told them not to eat and the serpent convinced Ewa to try it and Adam joined her. Since then we all have the same problem; we do things we should not do. Do you understand this?

Now please follow me to a time a few thousand years later when Hazrat Mosa was leading the people across the desert. This is found in the book of Numbers. The people began to complain. They complained about everything; the food, Hazrat Mosa, and even Most Merciful Allah. Then Allah sent fiery serpents and they bit the people and they died. Hazrat Mosa prayed and Allah told him to form a pole and fasten on it a bronze serpent , and to take the pole out and raise it up before the people and tell them I said to look upon it, and everyone who looks will live and everyone who is bitten and does not look will surely die. That is what happened exactly. Those who turned and looked lived, and those who didn't died. You may have seen this pole today on a hospital, or an ambulance. Now let's go on to zero to an event told about in the ancient scripture in the book of Yohana chapter 3. Hazrat Isa is 33 years old. It is a dark night and a man is coming up the road to the house. The man's name is Nickodemus. This man was a leader and teacher and he had a big question. Like us he wondered if he really would be accepted by Allah on Judgment day. He greeted Hazrat Isa and spoke to Him saying, I know you are from Allah because of all the wonderful things you do. Hazrat Isa then spoke Nicodemus, you can't even see the kingdom of Allah unless you are born again. What? said Nicodemus. How can I be born again, go back into my mother's womb and come out a second time? Hazrat Isa then tells him, "That which is born of the flesh is flesh, blood and water, but that which is of the Spirit is like the wind, you don't know where it comes from and you can't tell where it goes, so is everyone who is born of the Spirit. Then Hazrat Isa makes an amazing statement. Just as Hazrat Mosa lifted up the serpent in the wilderness, so must I the Son of man be lifted up that I may draw all men to myself. Dear friend it is time to personally see Him as our Saviour. He suffered the punishment we deserved then brought us back to a right relationship. He paid for all our sin. Will you turn against your sin and look with me to Hazrat Isa? Trust Him to take your burden and clean you from your sin? He alone offers us this eternal life. When you come to Him, He will come to you in your spirit. Yes, or no, will you look to Him and live? Please join me and pray for forgiveness and a new life.

Appendix 3:
Eight Special Signs Were Given to Seven Major Prophets

Overview

The first sign is about the Holy Books. The 2nd and 3rd signs, the garment of righteousness and the ark, show us that man could only escape the penalty of shame and sin by Allah's provision, not by his own good works. The 4th and 5th signs, sacrifice and blood, show us how Allah used them to save people from death. The 6th sign, the Psalms, are a sign of the coming Messiah because they tell about him hundreds of years before he was born. We also saw that the Messiah was to be a descendant of David. The 7th sign, the sign of Jonah, also seems to be pointing to the Messiah. Now let's take a look at the 8th sign, Jesus the Messiah himself.

Eight Special Signs were given to seven major Prophets

A. The first three show us *what* Allah will do for us.

1. **Holy Books**…Moses, David, Jesus

2. **Garment of Righteousness**…Adam

3. **The Ark**…Noah

B. The next two show us *how* Allah will do this work.

4. **Sacrifice**…Abraham

5. **Blood**…Moses

C. The last three Signs show us *through whom* Allah will do this work.

6. **The Psalms**…David

7. **The Sign of Jonah**…Jonah

8. **Jesus the Messiah**…Jesus

Sign 8-Jesus

Let's summarize now the uniqueness of Jesus. Then we will summarize again briefly how Jesus fulfilled all 6 of the previous signs. Then we'll conclude with what this means for all of us.

Jesus is the only prophet:

Appendix 3

1) to be born of a virgin.
2) to be called the Word of Allah.
3) to be called a Spirit proceeding from Allah.
4) to do all the miracles he did.
5) to be called a holy son.
6) to be called a Mercy from Allah.
7) to be called the Messiah.
8) to be strengthened with the Holy Spirit.
9) to rise from the dead.
10) who will come back at the end of the world. He will then be the last prophet.

Once again in brief summary, how did Jesus fulfill the previous 6 signs? Jesus became our garment of righteousness so we could receive forgiveness from Allah and stand before Him in righteousness rather than all our sin. Jesus was our Ark (or boat) because he came to earth to save us from Allah's judgment of our sin, just like the boat saved Noah and his family from Allah's judgment on the sin of the world from the flood of water. Jesus was that momentous sacrifice, dying in our place so we could be forgiven and go to Paradise. It was Jesus' blood on the cross that keeps the angel of death from taking us to hell. Jesus is the promised Messiah, or Allah's anointed one. Just like Jonah was in the belly of the whale for 3 days and 3 nights, so was Jesus 3 days and 3 nights in the heart of the earth before he rose from the dead.

Just before we conclude, let's look at 12 more verses in the Tawrah:

Isaiah 53:1-12-Isaiah the Prophet wrote this about Jesus 700 years before He was born.

v.5-6-here we see that Jesus died because of our sins. The whole world's sins were laid on Jesus when He died.

v.7-here we see that Jesus was like a lamb. Indeed, He is the Lamb of God that takes away the sin of the world (John 1:29).

v.8-here again we see that Jesus died for the sins of the people. The people deserved the punishment for their sins, but Jesus took that punishment upon Himself in their place.

v.10-here we see that Jesus became a guilt offering for the sins of the world, just like the animals used to be guilt offerings for the people.

v.11-Jesus will bear the whole world's sins.

v.12-once more we see that Jesus poured out His life in death for us. He bore the sins of the whole world.

Again I want to emphasize that this was written 700 years before Jesus was born. This was foretold by Allah. Therefore, Jesus dying on the cross was not a shameful accident. It was the plan of Allah. Jesus had to die. Seven of these twelve verses teach that He died for the world's sins. He came into the world with that as His primary purpose. He was born that He might become that one final, momentous sacrifice for the sins of the world.

So what does all this mean for us? Because the human soul is prone to evil (Surah 12:53), we cannot earn our own way to Paradise. We can only get to Paradise by Allah's Mercy and forgiveness (Surah 7:23, 12:53). If not for His mercy, we shall certainly be lost. In Surah 19:21, Jesus is called the Mercy from Allah. Since Allah told Adam and his wife they would die if they ate from the forbidden tree, He must keep His promise and punish them. Allah does not lie. Since all men sin, they will all die and go to hell unless Allah gives us another plan. He did. He provided the sacrificial system in the Tawrah so animals could die for the sins of the people. Then when the people repented and sacrificed the animals, the peoples' sins were forgiven. But the problem here is that their death only brought forgiveness for past sins, not future. When Jesus came and died for our sins, He died for all the world's past, present, and future sins. Death was the penalty Allah required for our sins. Someone had to pay it. Jesus is the only one who did. That is why we must come to him to receive forgiveness to be able to go to Paradise when we die, because no one else ever died for man's sins. Jesus ended the animal sacrificial system. He was that last momentous sacrifice.

I was told that I needed to do the following:

1) believe that I had disobeyed Allah's laws and will
2) believe that I could not earn my own way to paradise
3) repent (choose, with Allah's help, not to do the evil things that I used to do, and not to continue pursuing this evil goal of seeking glory for myself).
4) believe that Isa Al-Masih died on the cross for the forgiveness of my sins
5) receive His forgiveness right now by faith
6) choose to follow Isa Al-Masih and surrender to His path for my life

After thinking about this for about 2 weeks, I made the decision to do the things they told me I must do in order to receive forgiveness from Allah. It was definitely the most important decision that I ever made. Since that day I have a different eternal goal now. The following are the main reasons why choosing to follow Isa Al-Masih was the most important decision I have ever made in my life:

1) **I now know for sure that when I die, I'm going to paradise forever.** I now no longer fear death.

2) **Allah loves me**. The greatest need I have in the world is for love. Allah is perfect love. He loves me, He forgives me, He helps me, He has compassion on me, and He tells me His plans for me.

3) **Allah now lives inside me**. Allah used to be far away from me. Now He lives inside me by His Holy Spirit. There is no one closer to me now than Allah.

4) **Allah gives me great joy because I no longer fear judgment because I know my sins are forgiven right now**. I don't have to wait for judgment day. I know my sins are forgiven right now.

5) **Allah is my best and closest friend**. I can share everything with Him. I can tell Him anything and He listens to me. He also tells me all the wonderful plans that He has for me.

6) **Allah hears and answers my prayers**. Two examples are from I Thessalonians 5:24 and Proverbs 19:17.

7) **The power of Allah's Holy Spirit**. Before I decided to follow Isa Al-Masih, I was weak because Allah's Spirit did not live inside me. I couldn't follow Allah's laws. Now, with Allah's Holy Spirit living inside me, I have power to obey His laws. Allah is helping to free me from problems that have bothered me most of my life.

Because of all the above reasons, you can see that following Isa Al-Masih is by far the greatest and most joyful life there is.

This is just a summary of the 8 signs – if you want to get the whole version of the 8 signs, please write to: youwillbeablessing@gmail.com

Appendix 4:
Jesus in the Quran and in the Bible

No.	Title in Arabic	Title in English	Quran	Bible
01	Kalimah Allah	Word from God	3:39; 3:45; 5:46, 110; 57:27; 4:171	John 1:1.14; Mark 1:14-15
02	Qawl al-Haqq	Word of truth	19:34	John 14:6; Eph 1:13
03	al-Haqq	The truth of the Lord	3:49; 3:60	John 1:48; 4:17
04	ar-Ruh	Spirit from God	4:171; 21:91	Mt 12:28; Luke 1:35
05	al-Masih	The Messiah	3:45; 4:157; 4:171; 5:17,72,75	Mt 16:16; John 1:41; 4:25-42
06	ar-Rasul	Apostle of God	2:87; 2:253; 3:49	Heb 3:1; Mt 10:40
07	an-Naby	Prophet or messenger of God	2:136; 3:49; 6:85; 4:163; 19:30; 57:27	Mt 21:11; Luke 4:24; John 5:30
08	al-Abd-Oullah	Servant of God	4:172; 19:30; 43:59	Mt 12:18; John 4:34; Mk 10:42-45
09	Ibnu Maryam	Son of Mary	3:45; 19:34; 43:57; 61:6	Luc 2:48
10	Ahya	The one who raises the dead	3:49; 5:110	John 11:38-44; Luke 5:21-43; Luke 11:17-44
11		has power to create	5:110	John 1:3; Heb. 1:1-14
12	as-Shahid	Witness (at the Judgment day)	4:41; 4:159	Mt 24
13	Rahmah	A Mercy from God	19:21	Mt 9:27-30
14	Hikmah	Came with wisdom	3:48; 5:110; 43:63	Luke 2:40.52; Eph 1:2-14
15	Waha/Wahy	The one who is inspired by God	4:163	Mt 3:16; Luke 4:18
16	Tanzil	The one who has received revelation from God	3:48; 19:30-34; 5:110; 57:27	Mt 3:17; Luke 9:35; John 7:16-18
17	Ayah	A divine sign for men	3:49; 19:21; 21:91; 23:50	Mt 2:2.9; Luke 2:8-35
18		Announcer of Judgment day; his return signals coming of judgment	43:61	Mt 24:37-38; Acts 1:11
19	Mathal	An example	43:57; 43:59	John 13:1-11
20	Ayah	A miracle maker	2:253; 3:49; 3:50; 5:110-115	Mark 1:34; 5:41-42; John 10:32

Appendix 4

No.	Title in Arabic	Title in English	Quran	Bible
21	Taba	The one we should follow	43:61	John 1:37; 10:27
22	Ta'a	The one we should obey	3:50; 43:63	Mt 17:5; Mark 1:27
23	Moubassira	The announcer of Good News	61:6	Mt 4:23; Luke 4:18
25	Salih	One of the Just (righteous)	3:39; 3:46; 6:85	Mt 27:19; 2 Tim 4:8
26	Alama	One who knows the Holy Books	3:48; 5:110	Mt 12:5; John 4:25
27	Kamathali Adama	The one who is like Adam	3:59	1 Cor 15:45; Rom 5:18
28	Gulaman Zakiyyan	pure, sinless	19:19	Luke 23:4.14.41; Heb 4:14-16
29	Muqarraba	One close to God	3:45	John 14:9-10; Heb 2:9
30	Jiha	Honored here and above	3:45	Phil 2:9-11; Eph 1:21
31	Mubaraka	The blessed of God	19:31	Mt 21:9; Luc 1:42
32	An'ama	One of God's favorite	5:110; 43:59	John 1:18; Mark 1:11
33	Ruh al-Qudus	One strengthened by the Holy Spirit	2:87; 2:253; 5:110	Mark 1:11; Luke 4:14
34	Sayyd	A chief	3:39	Mt 21:8-10
35	Hasur	A chaste	3:39	2 Cor 5:21; 1 Pet 2:22
36	Salam	A man of peace	19:32	Isa 9:5-6; John 14:27
37	Qaffa	The one sent by God	5:46; 57:27	John 10:36; 17:4
38	Lam Saquiyyan	The man of happiness	19:32.33	Mt 5:3-12
39	Misdaq	The Confirmation of the Thora	3:46.50; 61:6	Mt 5:17; John 1:45
40	Bayyinat	The one who brings doubtless proofs	2:87; 2:253; 43:63	John 12:37; 10:25
41	Rafa'a	The one who died and was lifted up to God, ascended to heaven	3:55	Mark 16:19; Acts 7:56; Phil 2:8-11
42	Abari	A healer	3:49; 5:110	Luke 9:37-43; Mark7:31-37; Luk 17:11-19
43		Born of a virgin	3:47; 19:20-22; 21:91; 66:12	Matt. 1:18-25; Luke 1:26-38

Appendix 5:
Chronological Bible Study – 44 Studies

Suggested Series of Bible Studies

Suggestion for a series of studies on the plan of God for our lives:
The way of salvation

Brief introduction: Origins and aims of the Holy Scriptures

Old Testament

A: Genesis

1. God creates
2. God and man; the garden of Eden; the two trees
3. God and the rebellion of man; its results; the provision and promise of God
4. Cain and Abel
5. God, Seth and Enoch
6. God and Noah; divine provision by judgement
7. God and the tower of Babel
8. Call and blessing of Abraham; Abraham and Lot; justification by faith
9. The sins of Abraham; Ishmael; the covenant with Abraham
10. God and Sodom and Gomorrah
11. God gives Isaac and provides a lamb
12. God and Isaac
13. God and Jacob
14. God and Joseph
15. God and Satan (his origin, his rebellion)

B: Exodus – Deuteronomy

16. God protects and calls Moses
17. The ten plagues and the Passover
18. God leads His people through the Red Sea
19. God's covenant; the Ten Commandments
20. God meets man in the Tabernacle; the sacrifices
21. God and the 10 spies, the rebellion of the people
22. God leads his people in the desert; the bronze serpent
23. God promises a prophet like Moses

C: Historical Books

24. God leads Joshua into the promised land
25. Short summary of Judges, Samuel, King David, Solomon

D: Various

26. God and Jonah
27. God promises a Saviour; the Psalms, Isaiah, Micah
28. Short transition towards the N.T.

New Testament

29. God announces the birth of John and of Jesus
30. God gives John and Jesus
31. Baptism and temptation of Jesus
32. Jesus announces his mission in Nazareth
33. The authority of Jesus over demons
34. The authority of Jesus over sickness and death
35. The authority of Jesus over nature
36. Teaching of Jesus: living God's way
37. The transfiguration of Jesus
38. Jesus criticises hypocrisy
39. Jesus teaches about life after death
40. The last supper of Jesus; the betrayal
41. Condemnation, crucifixion, death and burial
42. Resurrection, appearances, ascencion

The message of Emmaus

43. "Did not the Christ have to suffer?"
44. Who is Jesus?

Bibliography

CAMPBELL, WILLIAM, *Qur'an and the Bible in the light of history and science*, Middle East Resources, 1993

CHANDLER, PAUL-GORDON, *Pilgrims of Christ on the Muslim Road – Exploring a New Path Between Two Faiths*, Cowley Publications, 2007

ERIC, CHRISTEL, *Chronological Bible Storytelling – The gentle way to the heart*, Life Challenge Africa, 2002

GILCHRIST, JOHN, *Facing the Muslim Challenge*, Life Challenge Africa, 2002

GREENLEE, DAVID H., *From the Straight Path to the Narrow Way – Journeys of Faith*, Authentic, 2005

GREESON, KEVIN, *The Camel: How Muslims are coming to faith in Christ*, Arkadelphia, AR: WIG-Take Resources, 2007

LAI, PATRICK, *Tentmaking: Business as Missions*, Waynesboro, GA, Authentic Media, 2005

MARTIN, EJ, Editor, *Where There Was No Church – Postcards from Followers of Jesus in the Muslim World*, Fruitful Practice Research, Learning Together Press, 2010

NAJA, BEN, *Releasing the workers of the 11th hour – the global south and the task remaining*, William Carey Library, 2007

NEHLS, GERHARD AND WALTER, ERIC, *Christian-Muslim Controversy*, Life Challenge Africa, 2006

NEHLS, GERHARD AND WALTER, ERIC, *Islam – Basic Aspects*, Life Challenge Africa, 2005

NEHLS, GERHARD AND WALTER, ERIC, *Practical-Tactical Approach*, Life Challenge Africa, 2006

PARSHALL, PHIL, *Muslim Evangelism – Contemporary Approaches to Contextualization*, Gabriel Publishing, 2003

SCOGGINS, DICK, *Planting House Churches in Networks*, rev.ed Fellowship of Church Planters, 1995

SIMPSON, WOLFGANG, *Houses that change the world*, Authentic, 2001

SINCLAIR, DANIEL, *A vision of the possible*, Authentic Media, 2005

SWAERTLEY, KEITH E., *Encountering the world of Islam*, Authentic Media, 2005

WOODBERRY, DUDLEY, *From Seed to Fruit – Global trends, fruitful practices and emerging issues among Muslims*, WilliamCarey Library, 2008

Index of Figures

Figure 1:	The three sources for our strategies	13
Figure 2:	Islam is more than Religion	28
Figure 3:	Their social context	29
Figure 4:	The cycle of our communication	39
Figure 5:	Person of Peace Strategy: "Go" versus "Come"	64
Figure 6:	The person of peace	66
Figure 7:	Diagram of the way of salvation	82
Figure 8:	Confessions of authentic faith	94
Figure 9:	Physical and Spiritual birth	100
Figure 10:	The socio-spiritual environment of the new believer	103
Figure 11:	Three dimensions of teaching	106
Figure 12:	New fellowships of faith: Three basic activities	112
Figure 13:	Beginnings and first phases of the fellowship	116
Figure 14:	Avoid importing foreign church forms into Muslim communities	121
Figure 15:	Extracted and implanted believer	132

Index of Tables

Table 1:	The different types of people and how to approach them	31
Table 2:	An example of felt needs	38
Table 3:	Culturally appropriate vocabulary	45
Table 4:	Summary of the Tentmaker Strategy	58
Table 5:	Comparison of Religious concepts	73
Table 6:	The disciples of Emmaus	74
Table 7:	Basic biblical concepts	75
Table 8:	Five important influences during the conversion process	93
Table 9:	The phases of the process	93
Table 10:	Example of an inductive Bible study	108
Table 11:	Twelve advantages of house fellowships	119
Table 12:	Characteristics of a biblical faith community	127
Table 13:	Characteristics of a mature personality qualifying for leadership	130
Table 14:	Approaches that inhibit or accelerate growth	132

Bert de Ruiter

Sharing Lives

Overcoming Our Fear of Islam

This book argues that the single greatest hindrance to Christian witness amongst Muslims in Europe is fear.

Many European Christians fear that Europe will gradually turn into Eurabia, or Islamic domination of Europe, and they ignore the efforts of Muslims to adapt to the European context, a situation pointing to a future scenario of Euro-Islam, or Islam being Europeanized. The author argues that instead of an attitude of fear, which leads to exclusion, Christians should develop an attitude of grace, which leads to embrace.

After analyzing books and courses developed to help Christians relate to Muslims, he concludes that these mostly concentrate on providing information and skills, instead of dealing with one's attitude. Because of this the author developed a short course to help Christians overcome their fear of Islam and Muslims and to encourage Christians to share their lives with Muslims and to share the truth of the Gospel.

Pb. • XIII + 209 pp. • £ 13.95 • US$ 22.95
ISBN 978-3-941750-22-7

VTR Publications • Gogolstr. 33 • 90475 Nürnberg • Germany
info@vtr-online.com • http://www.vtr-online.com

Lightning Source UK Ltd.
Milton Keynes UK
UKHW02f0307050518
322131UK00005B/705/P